Who's been sleeping in my bed?

How to swap your home and enjoy
free holiday accommodation worldwide

Jackie Hair

Exile Publications

Published by Exile Publications
PO Box 8076 Angelo Street
South Perth WA 6151 Australia
www.iinet.net.au/~exile
email: exile@iinet.net.au

First published 2001

Printed by Lamb Print
Cover design by Robyn Mundy Designs
Illustrations by Louise C. Burch, Graphic Designer
Typesetting by Vida Corbett
Digital Imagery© copyright 2001 PhotoDisc, Inc.

National Library of Australia
Cataloguing-in-Publication entry

Hair, Jackie
    Who's been sleeping in my bed? : how to swap your home and enjoy free holiday accommodation worldwide.

    Includes index.
    ISBN 0 646 41533 6.

    1. Home exchanging. 2. Vacations. 3. Travel - Planning.
    I. Title.

643.12

DISCLAIMER This book is written in good faith to provide accurate information concerning the subject matter covered. While every effort has been made to ensure the accuracy and currency of the information, it may contain errors in content and the information provided may change. Readers are invited to contact the author with stories, comments and suggestions for future editions. The author and Exile Publications accept neither responsibility nor liability for inconvenience, loss, expense, damage or injury caused by relying on the information or advice in this book. Readers should check the current position with the relevant authorities before making personal arrangements.

ABOUT THE AUTHOR

Intrepid traveller Jackie Hair has journeyed through and observed life in over thirty-five countries from Costa Rica to Congo. In 1993, she founded the home exchange club *Latitudes Home Exchange*, arranging home exchange holidays for hundreds of families in over forty countries.

During her seven years running the busy international club, Jackie answered thousands of questions about home exchange and surveyed numerous families during and after their exchange holidays.

Drawing on this vast knowledge, Jackie has written the comprehensive guide *Who's Been Sleeping In My Bed?* to help you achieve your most treasured holidays through the exciting world of home swapping.

ACKNOWLEDGMENTS

The author wishes to extend sincere gratitude to the members of *Latitudes Home Exchange* who shared their invaluable experiences and suggestions to help others gain the most from their exchange holidays; to Carol Henderson for granting permission for the reproduction of sample listings and forms owned by *Latitudes Home Exchange* and to Vida Corbett of *Women in Publishing WA* for her generous support and guidance.

Contents

	Page
Introduction	1
What is Home Swapping?	**4**
What is home swapping?	4
How do I know that my home will be safe with 'strangers' living in it?	5
Will my home be good enough for my guests?	6
Will others want to come to my area?	7
How likely am I to secure an exchange?	8
When is the best time to go?	9
Which destinations are available?	10
For what length of time could I exchange?	11
Who are Home Swappers?	**12**
The Benefits of Home Swapping	**16**
Save money	16
Access free use of car	18
Experience authentic local culture	20
Maintain your independence	22
Undertake a fact-finding mission	22
Avoid kennelling fees through reciprocal pet care	23
Enjoy home comforts	24
Use the host amenities	24
Stay longer	25
Contribute to eco-tourism and choose the ideal holiday	26
Retain peace of mind	26
Additional benefits	27

Some Drawbacks of Home Swapping   28

Destination and timeframe constraints   28
Planning and communication requirements   29
Flexibility requirement   29
Variable house-keeping standards   30
Preparation requisite   31
Damage and breakages   31
Language barriers   31
Exchange plans falling through   32
Misrepresentation of incoming guests   35
Minor irritations   35

Swappers' Tales   36

Related Lodging Alternatives   45

Hospitality exchange   45
Homestay   47
Unsynchronised exchange   48
House-sitting offered   50
House-sitter wanted   50
Rental available   52
Youth hospitality exchange   52
Non-reciprocal exchanges   52
Consecutive exchange series   54
Transaction combination   56

How the Internet has Revolutionised Home Swapping   57

Getting Started   60

Planning ahead   60
Deciding whether to register with a
formal home exchange club   60
Friends and family   61
Advertising   61
Publishing a personal web site   62

Formal clubs 63
Finding the right home exchange club 80

Getting the Edge on Finding the Right Exchange Partners 85

Registering your interest 85
Expanding on your proposal 88
Identifying potential exchange partners 101

Communicating with Your Exchange Partners 103

How to get in touch 104
Communication tips 105
Sample letters and forms 106

Issues to Address with Your Exchange Partners 111

Meeting your guests 112
Maps 114
Keys 114
Telephone charges 114
Utility bill obligations 116
Use of household supplies 117
Mail handling 117
Linens and towels 117
Repairs and maintenance 117
Absences and additional guests 118
Home and contents insurance 118
Car exchange and insurance 119
Contingency plans 122
Pets 124
Gardening and plant care 125
Finalising dates and confirming airline bookings 126
Home Exchange Agreement form 126

Travelling with Children 130

Case Study 133

Preparing Your Home and Car for Your Exchange Guests 152

Compiling an information file   153
Making your guests feel welcome   163
House-keeping   164
Sentimental or valuable items   166
Linens and towels   166
Preparing your car   166
Pets   168
Preparing a second home   168
Provisions for an exchange series   168

Maintaining and Leaving Your Exchange Home in Good
Order   169

Looking after your exchange home   169
Leaving your exchange home in good order   170

When You Arrive Home   173

Disabled Travellers   175

Youth Hospitality Exchange   180

The benefits   182
Learning the language   183
How to arrange a youth exchange   184
Selecting a program   184
Preparation   185
Receiving credit for schooling   186
Hosting a youth   186
Formal program resources   187

Resources   192

Glossary   215

Index   219

Introduction

For the author, a home exchange club was born from a personal need. When Jackie and husband Bruce decided to move to Australia, they were unable to sell their homes in California due to a downturn in the real estate market at the time. So they rented out both homes. On arrival in Australia, asset rich and cash poor and not knowing with any certainty what life in Australia would have to offer, Jackie and Bruce were forced to become tenants themselves.

They found the regular property inspections intrusive and the whole experience of renting restrictive and a waste of finances. Back in California though, the property managers had started identifying more with their tenants than the owners and Jackie and Bruce seemed disadvantaged at both ends.

Experiencing the impact of the 'worst of both worlds', that is, being tenants as well as absentee landlords without any control, they wondered if there couldn't have been a better way to smooth the transition to their new life.

That's when they started thinking how easy life would be, instead of having a series of transient people living in their homes who obviously weren't going to look after them as their own, if they found an Australian family doing the same thing in reverse.

Could there be a Perth home owner who might want to use a 'real' home for twelve months while they explored the possibilities of life in California? Surely, someone in the Perth area would be moving to California at the same time, unsure of whether they wanted to stay permanently and also not wanting to 'burn their bridges before they crossed them'.

This is how the idea of home exchange was born. Jackie and Bruce began to research the topic and discovered that although the concept was popular in North America and, to a lesser extent in Europe, it was hardly known in Australasia.

They started discussing the idea with new acquaintances and the feedback was very positive. So they devised a market survey questionnaire and engaged some enthusiasts to approach unsuspecting shoppers in busy shopping malls to gauge the interest level. The response was so positive that they started a mailing list to register the high interest level.

A business opportunity was evolving. Bruce at the time was still visiting aircraft hangers scouting for work and trying to convince the Civil Aviation Authority that 12,000 flight hours, albeit earned outside Australia, still counted for some experience. Jackie needed a career change after nearly two decades working as an occupational therapist. They decided to take the plunge and registered the business name, *Latitudes Home Exchange.*

Not long after, the first customers joined the service and a database of potential swappers was started. In the seven years that followed, thousands of new members joined in over 30 countries. A network of branch offices was established in ten countries.

During the time spent researching the home exchange concept and subsequently running the busy home exchange club, Jackie and Bruce found virtually no literature to assist new members in successfully arranging and executing a home exchange. Only one book could be found on the subject and this appeared to be directed solely towards American audiences.

Members returning from exchanges were surveyed and a list of their recommendations and guidelines was compiled and improved over the years. These guidelines were circulated to all new members as they joined. Ultimately, just about any eventuality and any possible query from potential new members was covered.

The information in this book was compiled from the results of these extensive market surveys of novice and veteran exchangers and from the experience gleaned from seven years of owning and running the busy, international home exchange club.

This guidebook gives you as much information as possible and should help you to avoid overwhelming and daunting situations.

What is Home Swapping?

WHAT IS HOME SWAPPING?

*A*s the name suggests, home swapping is the reciprocal exchange of the use of homes by two parties for a temporary period. The participants decide the timeframe. The length of stay might be exactly the same for both parties, or one party may stay longer than the other.

In many cases, more than just the family home is exchanged and parties might make other amenities available to their guests. The most common accessory that comes with home swapping is the use of a car.

As you will discover, there are many variations on the basic transaction. The common characteristic is that both parties are offering some form of accommodation hospitality in return for a similar arrangement at their destination.

HOW DO I KNOW THAT MY HOME WILL BE SAFE WITH 'STRANGERS' LIVING IN IT?

The answer is that there are no guarantees in anything in life and nothing we undertake is totally without risk. It would therefore be less than honest to claim that home swapping is completely risk-free. Home swapping depends on trust and mutual understanding between the participants. Consider the following points:

Your potential exchange partners have taken some trouble to register their interest just as you have. They are probably proud home owners experiencing the same concerns as yourselves. Home swapping attracts stable, well-educated, caring people. There is trust, respect and understanding between the parties since you will be living in each other's home. This is a very different arrangement from tenant/landlord relationships where one party may feel they are 'owed' something by the other. By contrast, the benefits of home swapping are mutual.

There is no doubt that your home will be safer occupied than left vacant. Not only is it less susceptible to burglary, but any major system failure can be instantly detected and repaired. While you are away, you can have your gardens cared for, your mail collected and your house kept clean.

Complaints concerning wilful damage or neglect are virtually unheard of. Of course, accidents happen and occasionally some items may get broken. This usually causes more distress to the offending party than the owner and stories are told of people spending days shopping for replacement items only to find the original held no value for the owner whatsoever!

Many comments express the delight of how clean the home was on return and most have come to consider their exchange guests as friends. What begins as a business arrangement inevitably evolves into a strong friendship with mutual trust as its basis.

Members of formal clubs recognise the benefits afforded by the concept and few are willing to jeopardise that privilege.

WILL MY HOME BE GOOD ENOUGH FOR MY GUESTS?

Some people find photographs portraying 'typical' exchange homes quite intimidating. Will anyone want to come to our modest home? It was our experience that home-swappers do not place much importance on the actual value of the home, nor do they typically compare their home with that at the destination.

Many home-swappers are happy to exchange their large homes for more compact homes. After all, you aren't going on holiday to spend the entire time maintaining someone else's mansion and grounds.

The true value lies in the experience generated by the exchange, not in the comparative monetary value of the home itself. Swappers in the UK have exchanged sprawling manor homes for small townhouses in Sydney. A couple in New Zealand were delighted to exchange their electronically-gated mansion for a much smaller, cosy home in an English village.

You aren't going to *buy* the home, but use it as a base from which to discover authentic local culture in another country. Home exchange isn't for those who like the safety of 'no surprises'. These people opt for a hotel chain coupled with a steady diet from fast food outlets! Home swapping is for the adventurer. Even the most 'lived-in' home has more to offer your family than a stark, cramped hotel.

Provided your home is clean and tidy and you make sure there is adequate space for your guests to store their own belongings, it should be suitable for swapping.

It is important not to misrepresent your home and environs in any way. Make sure your prospective guests have a fair indication of what to expect. For example, if your home is under the flight path of a major airport, let your guests know in advance that they can expect some aircraft noise.

WILL OTHERS WANT TO COME TO MY AREA?

Many participants in rural locations have secured exchanges with parties who hadn't even previously considered their country as a destination. Not everyone likes a big city; many families enjoy bushwalking, integrating into a small village community, seeing the real 'outback' and generally getting off the beaten tourist track.

GREETINGS EARTHLINGS

Sue of Auckland, New Zealand took her family skiing in America. *"Our first two home exchanges have been a complete success. We swapped our home for homes in two ski destinations in Colorado. Our home exchangers came down for the Louis Vitton Challenger series and loved our home and environment. We even met the first one back while we were still in Colorado and skied Beaver Creek Mountain together."*

Veteran swappers Ken and June from the heart of the city of London welcomed a change of scenery. *"We thoroughly enjoyed our exchange trip to Katoomba in the Blue Mountains of New South Wales. It was a contrast to our other two exchange venues. The position of the house was excellent; a quiet and lovely location. It was excellently situated for touring and walking the local area."*

HOW LIKELY AM I TO SECURE AN EXCHANGE?

People who are open to the adventures that home swapping offers have a high probability of finding exchange partners.

Home exchange works best for those who have flexible dates and destinations and are open to offers. It works less well for those on strict time schedules with rigid destinations. A well-prepared proposal including photographs of your travelling party, your home and environs along with some interesting tourist information, may well prompt someone to consider your area who hadn't previously given it any thought.

WHEN IS THE BEST TIME TO GO?

One advantage of swapping is that, while more traditional forms of holiday accommodation are subject to excessive rate hikes during peak season, home exchange is unaffected by this trend. You can literally pick your timing as long as it suits both parties.

If you're retired and can travel anytime, it's best to go into home swapping with the idea of being completely flexible so that you can fit in with other exchangers' timeframe requirements. If you are able to do this, you will avail yourself of many more offers because many people have their holiday dates dictated by work or other commitments. People with very rigid dates have far less opportunities available to them.

With home swapping, there is really no 'best time' to travel. If you can travel off-season, you will avoid the crowds sometimes associated with popular destinations. And you might take advantage of lower airfares.

The population of swappers with school age children must travel during the school holidays. For overseas travel, this often means making use of the long summer holiday. In the Northern Hemisphere, this will usually be between July and September and in the Southern Hemisphere between December and February. If you're swapping within your own hemisphere, chances are that you will find plenty of families wanting the same dates. Those swapping across the hemispheres will need to be flexible with their timing.

If you do live in the Southern Hemisphere and the idea of a white Christmas and sipping brandy in front of a log fire in the local pub appeals to your sense of diversity, you will have a significant advantage in that there will be many home exchange opportunities available to you.

The same applies to those living in the Northern Hemisphere who must travel to the Southern Hemisphere during the northern summer months for whatever reason. Many exchange doors will open for you because that's when most swappers will want to come to your part of the world.

WHICH DESTINATIONS ARE AVAILABLE?

Home exchange is most widely used in Canada, USA, Britain, Western Europe and Australasia. Swapping opportunities exist to a much lesser extent in Africa, Asia and Eastern Europe. With the current trend of trading homes via the internet, many new places have been added to the list of home exchange destinations, some of which were virtually unheard of through more traditional means.

Opportunities for a great getaway may exist at your own back door. In addition to their overseas choices, many swappers have discovered that domestic exchanges can provide an ideal and inexpensive interstate or even intrastate break.

Many city dwellers welcome a weekend break to the country and country folk like to get into the cities every now and then. We found that some of our members living just a few hours drive apart found exchange partners with whom they swapped on a regular basis for weekends, holidays and the occasional break.

FOR WHAT LENGTH OF TIME COULD I EXCHANGE?

Determining the length of your exchange will be a matter of personal preference. An exchange can be just a weekend break or stretch to a full twelve months or longer. The average length of exchange is about four weeks. For overseas exchanges, the shortest recommended stay is ten days. Home swapping involves a great deal of planning and correspondence and it probably simply isn't worth it for a very short stay unless you are setting up an agreement whereby you will take advantage of a particular situation with the same exchange partners repeatedly.

Bob and Joy from Australia noted: *"We learned a lot from our first exchange. The most startling revelation was that anything over about four weeks in one location is a bit of a waste of time. We felt that after about one month in and around the south of England, we were ready to move on. We used the home as a base from which to explore other parts of England and Wales."*

If you are hoping to find employment at your exchange destination and are seeking a long-term stay, it is wise to investigate the length of stay permitted to incoming visitors by your own government. For example, many Australians have a legal right to live and work in England but the Australian Immigration Department rarely grants visas to incoming visitors of greater than six months duration. It may be possible for your guest to apply to extend their visa but this is unlikely to be granted until they are already in the country.

There is little point in holding out for a twelve month exchange if it is not legally possible for the other party to fulfil your request. If you desire one year overseas, you'll be better off listing your request as three to 12 months which will give you the opportunity to accept several shorter offers arranged consecutively.

Who are Home Swappers?

*H*ome swapping attracts responsible, well-educated people with an interest in broadening their horizons. They are families, singles, active retirees and professionals.

The concept lends itself well to retirees who may be on a fixed income with little spare cash for exotic holidays. Instead, they can use what is possibly their greatest asset, their home, to bargain for free accommodation all over the world. They can visit their children and grandchildren for extended periods while maintaining their own independence.

For those who are 'asset rich and cash flow poor', home swapping allows the home owner to use their real estate assets. This is a more cost-effective alternative to borrowing money against the equity in the home to pay for the holiday and then having to pay the interest on the loan.

Families travelling with children will appreciate having plenty of space for the youngsters to spread out, indoors and out, which is a lot more fun than being cooped up in a cramped hotel room.

You can swap with families who have children of a similar age so that age appropriate entertainment is already in place, whether that be outdoor swings, computer games or baby toys. If the weather isn't co-operative, there will be plenty of indoor activities available. Parents will still find room for some privacy.

Children may form instant age-related friendships in the neighbourhood and your hosts' babysitters can be made available to you. If your children are happy on holiday, you will be, too. If they aren't, you won't be either!

For the recently widowed, another form of exchanging homes known as hospitality exchange, offers a wonderful way to travel without experiencing the loneliness. As the term suggests, hospitality is offered by one party in return for reciprocal hospitality by the other party at a later date.

Sometimes it can be hard to get back in the swing of things after the loss of a long-term partner and an overseas trip might seem daunting to someone who hasn't yet fully adjusted to their new single life. Hospitality exchange offers a marvellous way of seeing the world as the guest of a local. The recipient is likely to be introduced to the host's own circle of friends with whom they can make lasting friends of their own.

For others, a sabbatical leave or temporary posting might be taking them to a new destination for several months. Home swapping allows them to move into 'home from home' accommodation while feeling secure about the safety of their own home and its contents.

When exchanging with others with similar disabilities, the disabled traveller has the assurance that the accommodation will be accessible and allow for maintenance of the maximum level of independence. The wheelchair bound traveller can slip into the life of the host with all the guesswork taken out of the arrangements. The host will be able to advise on such issues as accessible public transport, medical facilities, special parking facilities and a range of other facilities which might otherwise prove a barrier to the unfamiliar.

Since the advent of frequent flyer programs, many business travellers have accrued points for free air travel but find the cost of accommodation prohibitive when not part of a package holiday. Home swapping is the perfect solution.

Special interest groups can enjoy exchanging with each other. Whilst you can certainly swap with people outside your area of special interest, it is fun to exchange with people who share your own particular passion. This can include church groups, avid walkers, bird-watchers and sporting groups. If you seek a holiday which will allow you to indulge a particular interest, it is helpful to have a host who can provide expert advice and personal knowledge.

Home swapping lends itself well to particular professions such as those involved in the airline industry who may be able to travel at significantly reduced costs and to teachers who often enjoy extended holidays.

Home swapping can be suitable for just about anyone. To be eligible, all you need is a clean home and a desire to travel. Many swappers now have dozens of exchanges under their belts and can provide glowing reports and testimonials from their previous exchange hosts.

The following statistics are based on the membership of *Latitudes Home Exchange* over a seven year period. These findings are only a sample because results would vary somewhat from club to club depending on the specific markets targeted by the various home exchange organisations and the country where they are based. Figure 1 shows the percentage of members from each age group.

Figure 1. Breakdown of swappers by age group

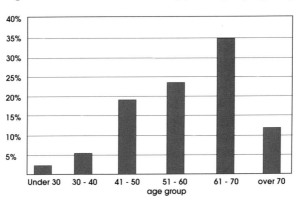

Figure 2 shows the percentage of members from various professions. In the category labelled 'other' we found architects, police officers, airline pilots, academics, attorneys, writers, farmers, engineers, clergymen, wool brokers and violin makers to name a few.

Figure 2. Breakdown of swappers by profession

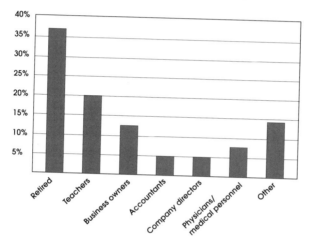

The Benefits of Home Swapping

*T*here are many advantages to home swapping and the extent to which you draw from these benefits depends on your individual circumstances. Home swapping allows you to:

Save money

Access free use of a car

Experience authentic culture

Maintain your independence

Undertake a fact-finding mission

Avoid kennelling fees through reciprocal pet care

Enjoy home comforts

Use the host amenities

Stay longer

Contribute to eco-tourism

Retain peace of mind

Enjoy a host of small gains

SAVE MONEY

The greatest benefit seen by most people is the tremendous savings in accommodation costs. Even renting an apartment in a city like London or Paris can run into thousands of dollars a week.

Using a very conservative approach, Table 1 shows how much an average couple might save on a two week holiday.

This takes into consideration that some meals will inevitably be purchased while sight-seeing and that exchangers will probably choose to sample some local restaurants, albeit at the recommendation of the exchange host who will be able to give advice based on personal experience.

The option to eat at home avoiding restaurant bills for three meals each day saves a lot of money. It is fun to visit local markets and take home fresh produce to prepare in relaxed surroundings.

Table 1. Comparative costs between home exchange and traditional accommodation

	Traditional holiday		Home exchange holiday	
Hotel accommodation	$100 per night	$1400		$0
Restaurants	lunch @ $10pp x 14	$280	lunch @ $10pp x 6	$120
	dinner @ $20pp x 14	$560	dinner @ $20pp x 4	$160
Weekly groceries		$0		$200
Car hire	$50pd x 14	$700		$0
Car insurance		$50		$0
Home swap club fees		$0		$125
Total cost		**$2990**		**$605**

pp = per person, pd = per day

As shown in Table 1, a couple might expect to spend around $2,990 on a traditional holiday compared to $605 on a house swap. This represents a savings of $2385 over a 14 day period.

You can adapt the same example to your own family by entering the estimated costs for additional family members in Table 2. These might include an extra hotel room for the children, the cost of extra meals or rental on certain equipment such as cot hire.

Table 2. Estimated holiday savings for our family

	Traditional holiday		Home exchange holiday	
Hotel accommodation				$0
Additional charges				
Restaurants	breakfast @ $__pp x __ days		breakfast @ $__pp x __ days	
	lunch @ $__pp x __ days		lunch @ $__pp x __ days	
	dinner @ $__pp x __ days		dinner @ $__pp x __ days	
Weekly groceries		$0		
Car hire	$__pd x __ days			$0
Car insurance				$0
Equipment hire				$0
Home swap club fees		$0		$125
Total cost		$____		$____

pp = per person, pd = per day

ACCESS FREE USE OF A CAR

"We were travelling on an unsealed logging track in the middle of the west coast of Vancouver Island when a black bear wandered over the road not thirty metres in front of the swapped car…"

Car hire represents another significant expenditure when touring overseas. More than 90% of swappers, recognising the tremendous savings, do exchange their cars. The exception being where both parties live in a city with excellent public transport such as Sydney or London and where taking to the roads by car is generally a frustrating exercise. It is still an advantage to have access to a car for trips further afield.

There are other benefits attached to swapping cars including convenience. If the length of time between the departing and incoming parties is not too great, it is possible for the outbound party to leave their car at the airport parking lot with prior instructions being given to the inbound members on how they can locate it. This would not be cost-effective for long periods as airport parking is notoriously expensive.

Where exchangers have arranged to overlap their stay by one or two nights, the incoming party can be met by the owners and taken to the exchange home to be shown around. Then, when it's time for the owners to depart, they can drive themselves to the airport in their own car with the guests taking the car back home. If the guests are very brave, they can chauffeur the owners to the airport!

A car can also be offered to balance inequities in length of stay. Bob of Launceston, Tasmania explains: "*Part of the arrangement was that, because our exchange partners were using our house for only four weeks, I agreed that they could have the use of one of my vehicles during their stay here. In return, we would have the use of their home for seven weeks but they couldn't offer the use of a car. So I hired one for seven weeks. 4000 kilometres later, it's fair to say, we had seen a great deal of the B roads, some of A and M roads as well. Oh yes, and plenty of ABCs (Another Bloomin' Castle).*"

EXPERIENCE AUTHENTIC LOCAL CULTURE

When you stay in hotels, you see the destination through the eyes of a tourist. You pay tourist prices. When you travel as a home-swapper, you live like a native experiencing authentic local culture. You have personal information on hand provided by your hosts.

You are part of the local community, usually becoming friendly with the neighbours, family and friends of your exchange hosts. This often leads to invitations of all descriptions to local events, sporting facilities, outdoor barbeques, informal gatherings or perhaps a branch of a club to which you already belong at home.

Many lasting international friendships have been made though home exchanges. Australians Bob and Joy are enthusiastic: *"One of the great spin-offs from our first exchange was that we met the neighbours. Right next door was a single Mum called Deb with a couple of children.*

One day Deb was in the front garden – a quaint English reference to a tiny strip of lawn between the road and the front door – struggling to landscape some rocks. This girl clearly wasn't from the bush. I told her to move over and let me at it.

An hour or so later, a bloke appeared from across the road with a rake. "Give you a hand, old man?" While I did the hard work, Lionel (a retired fireman) went away and bought some lawn seed. We tidied up the yard, got rid of the 'twitch' and prepared the ground for a new lawn.

Deb, I think, was somewhat overcome. Until the Aussies came along, she had never even spoken to her neighbours. Now Lionel not only tends the lawn, he mows it, too.

That was four years ago and, after repeated invitations, the guy with the rake has finally come to Tasmania to stay with us along with his wife Pauline. They had a holiday on the Barrier Reef and stayed with us for two weeks, thoroughly enjoying themselves.

It's funny that we have hardly ever heard from our UK exchange partners, but their neighbours keep in touch regularly. Deb still sends her greetings via Lionel's occasional missives."

John and Pat of Richmond, Yorkshire on an exchange to visit their daughter now living in Australia reported: *"We're meeting lots of locals that we wouldn't have otherwise met. It's crowded at our daughter's house with the children. And we're saving heaps."*

Similarly, John of Caloundra, Queensland said of his exchange to Horsmonden, Kent: *"It was an enjoyable way to travel which gave us a base or resting place between trips to other areas. We met neighbours and other locals. It was also a very cost-effective way for us to travel, particularly having a car to travel around the UK."*

Cultural differences aren't restricted to speakers of different languages. One Australian couple had this to report about cultural differences when swapping in England: *"The first major overseas exchange was with an English couple who had been swapping for years. I'll call them Adam and Eve (only part of which is correct).*

These folk met us on arrival from London by bus in the South of England and not only introduced us to the quaint Dorset accent, but also gave me a completely new understanding of the term '2 up'.

Prior to that trip, I had always thought '2 up' was the game played behind the Sergeants' Mess on Anzac Day. Not so for these delightful English. Their '2 up' was the bedroom and bathroom upstairs of their two-storey house. 2 up, 2 down and no room to swing a cat in any of it. Welcome to a British tenement house – home base for the next seven weeks.

But ideal just the same. Clean and tidy, with no backyard – or front yard for that matter - to worry about. We did England and Wales from that base."

MAINTAIN YOUR INDEPENDENCE

Home swapping allows people to visit relatives and friends without being a burden. No matter how sound the relationships or how exciting the visit from the overseas relatives may seem in the planning stage, these relationships inevitably become strained over a period of months, weeks, or even days in some cases!

The visiting relative will appreciate being able to entertain their family and friends or invite casual acquaintances over for a cuppa. This is generally not possible when you are a guest yourself.

Some families simply don't have room to accommodate the extended family and an exchange home in close proximity provides the ideal solution.

UNDERTAKE A FACT-FINDING MISSION

Exploring an area for potential migration, retirement or re-location can be very difficult through the eyes of a tourist. It's hard to get an appreciation of an area in a short period of time or when staying in hotels.

Home exchange allows people to experience an area as a local but without burning their bridges at home. If, by the end of your stay, the area hasn't lived up to your expectations, you can just return home and re-think your strategies.

AVOID KENNELLING FEES THROUGH RECIPROCAL PET CARE

Allowing your pet to remain at home in its familiar surroundings has several benefits. The pet will undoubtedly be happier than it would in a kennel. For longer trips, the cost of kennelling would be prohibitive. If your pet happens to be a guard dog, it can continue to protect your property while you're away.

Ideally, you would swap with a family who are also seeking pet care. They will be familiar with the routines and responsibilities associated with pet ownership.

Families who don't own a pet themselves may welcome the opportunity to expose their children to living with an animal and all that it entails, knowing that at the end of the holiday the responsibility is handed back to the owner.

Many exchangers are happy to care for smaller animals such as an independent cat. It is important to declare at the outset if you do own a cat because many people are allergic to them and might not be able to live in your house with or without the animal in residence.

ENJOY HOME COMFORTS

After a long day sight-seeing, it can be very relaxing to return to the comforts of home where there are books to read, toys to play with and comfy chairs to sit in. If rain stops play for a whole day or you want a day to unwind, you'll have plenty of room for children to spread out. Everyone can make a snack without having to plan an expedition to find something that appeals to everyone.

Max and Shirley of Eden Hills, South Australia had this to say about their month spent in a London exchange home: *"The experience of living in London in such a great position was terrific. In our opinion exchanging homes is the only way to go. This method of staying overseas is not only the best financial way to do it, but is also the most relaxing way."*

USE THE HOST AMENITIES

Swapping your home with like-minded people means that you may have many common interests. If you're a golfer, you may receive a personal introduction to your host's golf club. The option to swap golf clubs makes travelling considerably lighter. Members can arrange a library card, temporary gym membership, 'two for one' dine-out and entertainment books and access to a host of facilities that would not be available to you as a tourist.

Many members offer use of their recreational toys such as campervans, boats, windsurfers, bicycles and a wide range of other amenities.

The benefits to anyone who has experienced the rigors of travelling with babies will be immediately obvious. Packing and travelling will again become a simple matter. There is no need to hire or lug all that bulky equipment such as car seats, portacots, high chairs and the range of paraphernalia that small children require. Chances are, your exchange hosts will have all the same equipment available or they may have friends and family who can loan it to you.

Provision of additional amenities can be offered to balance out transactions if there are inequities in the length of stay or perhaps the type of accommodation being exchanged.

To accommodate a disparity in the required length of stay between the two parties, Peter of Capel-le-Ferne wrote to his potential exchange partners kindly offering the following solution:

"At the moment, we find ourselves in the position of being able to offer an exchange for only two months during May and June. However, we do have a two-berth caravan which we would be willing to tow and leave on any site anywhere. You would pay the site fees. Or we could loan you a car with the caravan, enabling you to travel around at your leisure during the month of July.

You could of course leave anything you didn't wish to take with you in the caravan in our safe-keeping returning for anything needed in between time whenever necessary.

This would give you the opportunity of being in England for the full three months and us to be away for only the two months which is all the time we can spare at the moment."

This form of generosity is common among the home exchange population.

STAY LONGER

Because home-swappers save so much on their accommodation, they can generally afford to stay in an area longer. They have more money to spend on excursions, side-trips and tourist attractions. They may join local clubs, a sporting facility or special interest group.

CONTRIBUTE TO ECO-TOURISM AND CHOOSE THE IDEAL HOLIDAY

As a home-swapper, you can feel proud that you are making a personal contribution to eco-tourism. No form of tourism could be more sustainable than one in which as one family arrives in an area, another family leaves.

Exchange homes are not necessarily located in areas associated with high-density tourism. This means that the incoming tourist dollars are more evenly spread throughout the local economies of smaller communities rather than being pumped only into the hotel coffers of large cities. Because they do stay longer, home swappers spend money on everyday items such as groceries and petrol.

Exchange homes are often located away from the beaten tourist track. Choose a village, beach, urban or mountain holiday. The range is limited only by your imagination.

RETAIN PEACE OF MIND

No value can be placed on the reassurance and peace of mind that comes with knowing that your home is secure in your absence. Although, in a sense, your exchange guests are strangers, you can feel safe in that the relationship is one of mutual trust and respect. This is quite different from the relationship experienced between landlord and tenant.

Home-swappers tend to respect each other's property and treat it as their own. Sue from New Zealand remarked of her first two exchanges in America: *"Both couples were very respectful of our material goods and equally friendly and helpful."*

You know where to find the exchange guest if something does need addressing after the exchange. If you've found your exchange partners through a home swapping club, they are unlikely to do anything in or to your home that could jeopardise their club membership in the future.

ADDITIONAL BENEFITS

There are many other small gains in swapping homes, one being that there is no need to carry valuables around with you all day when you go on sight-seeing trips. No need to risk leaving your passports and valuables in a hotel room or depending on the staff being available when you need access to the hotel safe.

You'll be able to think of many extra advantages yourself.

Some Drawbacks of Home Swapping

*A*sk most home-swappers about the disadvantages of home swapping and they'll probably look vague and draw a blank. For most, once experienced, this becomes a way of life.

Problems of any significance rarely occur. But there are some drawbacks unique to home swapping which include:

Destination and timeframe constraints

Planning and communication requirements

Flexibility requirement

Variable house-keeping standards

Preparation requisite

Damage and breakages

Language barriers

Exchange plans falling through

Misrepresentation of incoming guests

Minor irritations

DESTINATION AND TIMEFRAME CONSTRAINTS

You may not be able to get the destination of your first preference. Home exchange is not the same as booking a room in a hotel where you can determine availability and secure your reservation. You must rely on finding someone at your destination who wishes to come to your area, usually, at the same time you wish to travel and for the same length of time.

It therefore works best for people with flexible timeframes and open destinations.

Sid and Maureen from Sydney filed the following report on return from their four week exchange in Clayton, Sussex: *"You need to be very flexible with the exchange destination. Our exchange turned out really great even though it was nowhere near where we originally wanted to go. It will go down as one of our best holidays ever."*

PLANNING AND COMMUNICATION REQUIREMENTS

Home swapping involves considerable planning and correspondence. Once identified, you need to allow adequate time to correspond with your exchange partners. There are many issues requiring discussion and agreement and this takes some effort from both parties.

You will want to feel comfortable with these strangers before turning over your house and car keys to them. For this to happen, you need to take some time getting to know each other through correspondence and phone calls.

Before any of this can occur, you must spend time identifying the home exchange company you wish to join, preparing details of your home and area, taking photographs and finding the right people to swap with you. Of course, once you've prepared all this information, the task becomes much easier with subsequent exchange quests.

FLEXIBILITY REQUIREMENT

There can be difficulties in trying to co-ordinate dates and timing between different hemispheres where seasonal variations have to be considered. This may prove to be a limiting factor in finding those desiring your area at the same time. If, for example, you live in northern England, you will find that many potential swappers don't relish the thought of spending the months of January to March in your area for the very reason that you wish to escape. It is understandable that those coming from the Southern Hemisphere may not be attracted to experiencing three winters in a row. So, it will be necessary to show some consideration to the incoming visitor in order to make your offer more attractive.

VARIABLE HOUSE-KEEPING STANDARDS

Novices tend to be concerned about all the wrong things – theft and damage are virtually never encountered. Potential problems are more likely to be related to variations in house-keeping standards and expectations. What is spotless to one family may not be so to another.

Varying house-keeping standards and issues of cleanliness can distress some people. No two families will be the same in this regard.

PREPARATION REQUISITE

It takes some effort to adequately prepare your home for your exchange guests. You won't be able to just walk out and lock up as you could when leaving for a conventional holiday.

Levels of preparation for the exchange will vary. It can be disheartening to put a lot of time and effort into ensuring your guests have the best possible experience, only to find they've done very little in preparation for your own arrival.

DAMAGE AND BREAKAGES

Occasionally items get accidentally damaged or broken. Home swappers must be prepared to accept this.

LANGUAGE BARRIERS

Misunderstandings can arise between any two parties negotiating an exchange but are even more likely to occur when there are language barriers.

It is generally accepted that most people embarking on a home exchange holiday can speak at least some of the language of the destination country. English is widely spoken among home exchangers. If you're going to a non-English speaking country, it's obviously an added bonus if you can speak and understand the language.

In arranging the details of any exchange, good communication is essential and where the participants do not share a common language, it is even more important to spell out all the details of the arrangements as clearly as possible.

Jack of Victoria came to this realisation when he swapped his Point Lonsdale, Victoria home for one in Switzerland. *"The Swiss family either misunderstood the arrangements or the arrangements had* not been made clear enough to them. I tend to think that they are not particularly reliable and are not used to adhering to arrangements. Our agreed exchange was for four people to use our house for one month with a car provided by both parties.

But, when we arrived, two of the family who were supposed to be in Australia were still in residence. Fortunately the situation was resolved satisfactorily as we were able to stay elsewhere for five days until we could take up residence. No car was available for our use in Switzerland.

The number of people coming to our house kept changing, all arriving on different dates! Some of them wanted to stay on at our house for an extra four weeks but we could not agree to that. We agreed to an extra 10 days of which they took advantage.

In future we would not deal with a family where English could not be properly understood. We would tend to make arrangements with people in our own group. It was a learning experience and apart from the frustration at the time, we quickly got on with things and enjoyed our holiday very much."

A significant advantage of selecting a home exchange club which offers custom matching services is that the foreign club counterpart will prove very helpful in translating all the preliminary details of the exchange for its non-English speaking members. This should give you a head start when exchanging with people for whom English is a second language.

EXCHANGE PLANS FALLING THROUGH

Even with the best of intentions, plans occasionally get cancelled at the last minute due to circumstances beyond control such as ill-health or sudden death.

Once a firm exchange agreement has been made, backing out obviously causes considerable disappointment and inconvenience to the other party. Doing so without very good cause is unacceptable practice. Each party should assume responsibility for considering what alternatives you could offer your guests if *you* were forced to cancel the arrangements, rather than focusing on what would happen if the *other* party cancelled.

We know of one English lady who became seriously ill just four days prior to the intended departure to Australia. Rather than ruin the holiday for the incoming Australians, her husband decided not to mention that they would be unable to travel. He met the two sisters at London airport as arranged.

During the drive home, he explained that his wife was in hospital recovering from surgery and they would not be able to undertake the journey to Australia for the foreseeable future. He assured the Australians that they were most welcome to stay.

The Australians were, at first, uncomfortable with this idea since the planned exchange was for a period of six months. They knew their welcome would be worn out long before then. To their surprise, it did turn out well for several reasons.

The house was large enough to accommodate the visitors without them feeling as though they were getting in the way. As the lady was in hospital for some time, the guests provided excellent companionship and support for her husband. Because there was a second car available, the Australians were able to take themselves off to other parts of the UK for varying lengths of time to give everyone a break.

The Australians did return home earlier than originally planned but not before strong friendships had been forged and an open invitation had been given for the English couple to enjoy reciprocal hospitality in Australia at a mutually agreeable future date.

Although not ideal, and certainly not a common situation, it highlights the sense of responsibility of exchangers once a commitment has been given, even in the face of adversity.

Later, the husband, Jack, had this to say about the experience: *"Events certainly overtook any plans that had been made and it is quite a long story. Quite suddenly, Rita was diagnosed as having angina. As our home is quite a large house with five bedrooms, we were able to accommodate the ladies. My wife had a successful operation and was improving all the time but naturally she was not allowed to fly. Shortly afterwards, Gwenda and Rona arrived.*

For our part, we could not be sharing a house with two more pleasant and interesting ladies. There have been – from our point of view – no problems at all and we have really enjoyed their company in between their various visits to other parts of Britain. This has been some compensation to us for not being able to complete the exchange since we would not otherwise have met them.

We live in hope of another visit to Australia some time."

If you found your exchange partners through a formal club, the club may be able to help you find a substitute at short notice, especially if you've chosen a company noted for its personalised service. In their database they may have members who have been unable to secure an exchange or who have joined only recently, for example.

Bob and Joy of Tasmania were able to take advantage of a substitute when their planned exchange couldn't go ahead.

"We arranged a swap with a couple from Western Australia. But just when we were due to go to W.A., we had some serious illness in the family which forced us to travel to Queensland instead. Our exchangers came to our house but we were never able to take up our portion of the swap. Aware of the situation, our home swap club later arranged a subsequent exchange for us at no extra cost with another couple in the same area."

It is important to understand that you should not rely on the club for this assistance. The responsibility is your own and that of your exchange partner. Remember that some clubs, particularly internet-based only clubs, offer no such personalised assistance so this should be taken into consideration when selecting a club to join.

MISREPRESENTATION OF INCOMING GUESTS

An issue that confronts only a few exchangers is the misrepresentation of the number and age of arriving guests.

MINOR IRRITATIONS

And then there are those inevitable little mishaps. Those minor irritations that arise with any form of travel do apply to home swapping as well. Usually these little unexpected surprises make the best stories and create the lasting memories of travel of any kind.

Dora of Buderim, Queensland has this advice for would-be swappers: *"Go for it, you cannot lose, weighing the pros and cons, even with minor problems, you cannot afford not to do this. It is important to communicate with your exchange partners prior to departure."*

Dora and husband John spent six weeks in Bolton, England. Dora says: *"Our exchange experience was great. A wonderful idea to have a base to travel from and the use of an exchange car was an added bonus."*

You need to keep an open mind to all these things and consider that even in the worst case scenario that you can imagine, you're probably *still* better off by swapping.

Swappers' Tales

WESTERN AUSTRALIA – WALES

*R*ob and Betty swapped their Perth, Western Australia house for a farmhouse on the Welsh border. This was their fourth home exchange, their second to the UK.

"After a good flight and impressive service with Royal Brunei Airlines, we arrived at Heathrow in August 1997 in the height of England's summer. Our exchange destination was Bredwardine, a small village in the county of Herefordshire, very close to the Welsh border and near the Black Mountains.

Some four hours later travelling by car, we found the local pub, The Red Lion in Bredwardine, which proved to be the hub of the small village settlement. There were none of the customary rows of houses that we had passed on our way, and we soon realised that we were in a farming community with narrow winding lanes, wide open paddocks and hawthorn hedges for fences.

We found the signpost leading to our exchange house and started our climb upwards looking for a house name. There was no street name and no house number. Latitudes Home Exchange *had provided us with maps and photographs so, using these, we went looking up and down hills, only to realise we had the map upside down. "Ah, there it is! I recognise it from the photos".*

Jane, our exchange partner, has been living in Perth for some years and by exchanging her lovely farm house with Australian exchangers, she gets to experience our local culture and we hers in a way seldom experienced through conventional tourism.

A big wooden gate was the entrance to our 'home from home'. We soon found out that to leave the gate open was to run the risk of having neighbouring sheep and cattle in your front yard. We were pleasantly surprised by the size of the house. From every window upstairs you could see a wonderful vista, the River Wye winding through farmlands and the whole Wye Valley right on your doorstep. We never tired of looking at the scene and picking out landmarks – the church spires in the distance, now where was that?

The house itself is made of stone, 12 inches thick in parts, with stone floors covered by lovely rugs and carpet squares. The main bedroom is very large and all are nicely decorated with wash basins in two of them. The main bathroom upstairs has a separate shower – a rare find in England – a bath, basin and toilet with lots of cupboards with linen, etc. On the ground floor is a large dining room with lovely antique dresser and table and carver chairs, a lounge with its own fireplace and comfy lounge and chairs.

The kitchen is large, cosy and well equipped. Above the large Agar stove are wooden rails on pulleys over which you can hang all your washing and hoist it up to the ceiling. There is a large separate laundry, another rarity in England most forming part of the kitchen, a huge chest freezer and laundry sink. All in all it is a delightful setting. Falling off to sleep with the sounds of the lowing of cattle and awakening to the bleating of sheep makes it an idyllic place, the peace and tranquillity music to your ears.

Being high summer, we made the most of the long daylight hours and went exploring each day. Crossing into Wales, we found each village would have a different market day, so there was always an abundance of fresh vegetables, fruit, fish and meat. Whatever the title, you would be sure to find it among the wonderful books in the Hay-on-Wye bookstore.

Abergavenny has a wonderful market place and, after shopping, you can go to the pub 'Britannia' for a scrumptious lunch with a guest organist playing all the old songs every market day. We were warmly *greeted and it wasn't long before 'Waltzing Matilda' was struck up and everyone joined in the singing.*

Kington, another nearby village has gift shops and lovely cream teas and scones. Ross-on-Wye, set on a steep hill, has the usual church steeped in history. Country life is very laid back and it is nothing to be in a queue of twenty vehicles behind a tractor with a wide trailer full of potatoes being taken to market, everyone patiently crawling along the winding lanes while the tractor chugs its slow pace along in front.

Bredwardine is not a village with any facilities; supermarkets or major stores, British Rail and National Express terminals are all situated about 15 miles away in Hereford. A taxi will take you to the terminals for £15. Alternatively, you can leave your car at the rail station for a few days and it will still be there when you return.

The local shop at Peterchurch is easily reached by car in 10 minutes and has milk, bread, papers and small goods available. Bredwardine has no restaurants as such but there are many pubs in the immediate area that offer fabulous meals, especially roast beef and Yorkshire pudding on a Sunday.

Being a retired couple, we did not do a lot of walking due to the hills but a younger, more fit couple would have no difficulty exploring. There are stiles in the gaps of hedges with signs telling you where you can walk. Everyone is very friendly and will wave and greet you.

We were able to leave the house unattended for 10 days to do a tour of Scotland and The Lake District. Bed and Breakfast (B&B) accommodation proved more expensive than on our last visit but they were clean and good value and the people friendly. Swapping our home enabled us to stay overseas longer and have money to spare for such side trips.

We worked our way up the west coast and as far north as Inverness then down the east coast to York and back through Manchester to Hereford, the main town and back to the farm. We also went to Ireland flying from Heathrow to spend four days in Dublin before touring the

Ring of Kerry. We found the history of Ireland fascinating with the rise out of poverty and the potato rebellion when Ireland lost half its population to migration or starvation. Only recently have people started returning to Ireland, many of them being under 25 years old.

Back on the farm it's getting pretty cold by now and we dress to go to bed. The house has plenty of warm bedding. Many days of fog, mist and rain followed, referred to by the locals as 'mizzle', a combination of all three. As the days grew shorter with darkness arriving around 4.30 p.m., we were always happy to be home by that time and would light the fire in the lounge and sit together watching TV, playing cards or doing jigsaw puzzles. The cosiness of the wood fire with its leaping flames was very restful.

We left in mid-December with a feeling of sorrow. We'd enjoyed the countryside, the absence of the multitudes, the narrow twisting lanes and hawthorn hedges, the cattle and sheep, the marvellous hills, valleys, villages and scenery."

SOUTH PERTH – DIDCOT

Derek and Diane, also from Western Australia, swapped their home for one in Oxfordshire, England. The exchange was for ten months.

"We were aware of the concept of home swapping so when we decided to travel to England, we contacted the local club offering the custom matching service and they soon put us in touch with the couple that we ultimately exchanged homes with.

Derek had been to the UK before but for me and our two sons, it was our first time and we wanted to work and experience life there as a family.

Before we left we had the usual concerns and fears such as what if the people abused our home; what if the exchange house was located in a bad area; what if we were forced to return home earlier than planned and the people who were in our house were unwilling to leave. We needn't have worried.

The son-in-law of our exchange partners picked us up at London airport at 6 a.m. for which we were very grateful.

Our first impression was one of shock. Apart from the fact that we had bad jet lag, the house was a lot smaller than ours, but after no time at all, we found it to be very comfortable and it had everything one could have wanted right down to great neighbours. The hospitality from the friends, neighbours and family of our exchange hosts was tremendous. We became really good friends with a lot of the people we met there.

Although the styles and layout of the two homes were totally different, it made no difference to the way we lived and it was a great home for our family. Didcot was a great base and we travelled extensively within England from the Isle of Wight to Northern Scotland and places of interest to us on the west coast of England and Northern Wales.

Before our departure from Australia, we weren't told that Didcot had a power station on the edge of town. It was a shock seeing such a monstrosity, but it proved a very good landmark and you could see it for miles. We grew to love it.

We did a lot of fun things as a family. We went to so many steam train days in the UK that by the end of the trip, I hoped I'd never see another steam train!

On one outing, our car caught fire and was burnt out – along with 70 others – at a Civil War re-enactment at Witney. Luckily no-one was injured and our car was fully insured. I am sure our exchange partners are very thankful that we didn't exchange cars!

Home swapping provides an enormous cost-saving, particularly when you swap for many months as we did. An additional benefit is the knowledge that your house is being lived in and looked after by another home owner similar to yourselves.

We would like to return to England one day for another visit but we don't have any desire to live there. If the right opportunity presents itself, we'd exchange again."

DIDCOT – SOUTH PERTH

Derek and Diane's counterparts were Bob and Joyce, a retired couple wanting to spend an extended period of time with their son who had emigrated to Australia. They had just returned from a two month visit and had made up their minds to return for a longer period. They had already spent several weeks trying to work out the best way to achieve this goal when they spotted a small advert in a national newspaper for a home exchange to South Perth.

Both couples wanted to leave as soon as possible so the ensuing weeks were quite hectic putting everything in place. Bob explains how it worked out:

"Both families initially had some anxious times about the exchange but these were all ironed out during the planning stages. After a few reassuring phone calls, we felt like friends.

It was suggested that we arrange our flight to arrive two days before Derek and Diane's departure. This enabled us to spend a whole day familiarising ourselves with features of the home such as the swimming pool pump and the 'reticulation system'. We agreed on the procedures for bill payments at each other's home and both parties honoured these written agreements.

We had a wonderful and sometimes unbelievable adventure. We walked more than we did at home but after a short time, we bought a small used car and travelled thousands of kilometres in it. In the winter, we drove north visiting Kalbarri National Park, Carnarvon and Monkey Mia where we swam with wild dolphins, Coral Bay and Exmouth. We borrowed our son's camping gear and spent most nights in a small tent. In the summer, we went south towards Esperance almost getting lost in the bush on one occasion.

We also spent two unforgettable weeks at the homes of the parents of our exchange partners, Derek and Diane. Derek's parents, Jim and Joyce, live in a small country town called Mukinbudin. They took us around the local places of interest, showed us sheep-shearing and took us to an Aussie football match. Diane's parents, John and Pat, live on a farm in Southern Cross, not far from Kalgoorlie where Paddy Hannan first discovered gold. We drove round the vast farm, helped with hay-making and visited gold mines.

We remain good friends with both sets of parents. We have since returned to stay with one of the couples and they plan to use our home as a base when they come to England next year. Our own daughter, who was left in charge of our affairs in England, became very friendly with our exchange partners while they lived in our house and they have also remained in contact with each other.

The whole venture was more than a holiday. We actually lived in Australia. We spent Christmas Day at a neighbour's garden party, sitting in our shorts in the sunshine. We played bowls practically every week and played in three different bridge clubs making numerous friends with whom we still keep in touch. The cost of living balanced out with some items being more expensive and others cheaper than in England.

We could never have done half the things we did if we'd been stuck in a hotel. We had a lovely place to stay and met real people who turned our holiday into an adventure. Home exchange for us was a wonderful, not to be missed experience."

PERTH – TASMANIA

Two sets of members with a healthy sense of one-upmanship style humour were perfectly matched. John and Louvain of Perth, Western Australia were swapping with Bob and Joy from Launceston, Tasmania.

Bob and Joy had graciously offered to collect John and Louvain from the airport. Unfortunately, it was later revealed that their travel agent had booked them to arrive at Hobart airport, a 400 kilometre round trip from Launceston! The ticketing structure was such that the destination could not be changed.

Bob and Joy decided to honour their original offer and set off for the day excursion to Hobart airport. Bob had sent details of the meeting strategy with a description of himself and Joy a few weeks earlier. *"I suggest we meet at the Avis car counter within the Ansett terminal at the airport. You'll know us by our two heads and we both wear tinted glasses. Joy is 5 foot nothing with brown hair (thanks to regular trips to the hairdresser) and I am 5' 9" and don't need to go the barber very often at all.*

If, however, something unforeseen occurs en route to the airport and you can't locate us, ring my sister Margaret's phone number in Hobart. She will activate Plan B. Hopefully this won't be necessary."

On arrival at Hobart airport, the visitors knew they'd found the right couple when they saw the sign they were holding, "Sandgropers report here".

Bob wrote: *"Proud of our lovely environment, we met them intent on showing our hospitality. We dined together the first night, showed them around our house and gave them some local tips, tourist brochures and maps. The next day, we handed over the keys to our house and car and went to the airport headed for 'Sandgroper Territory'.*

In Perth, we were met by their son-in-law and driven to the exchange home, shown the ropes and given the keys to house and car. We had a wonderful three weeks in Western Australia, arriving back in Tasmania in time to spend one more evening with our guests.

We enjoyed swapping stories over dinner and a couple of glasses of wine before taking them to the airport the following morning. This time though, I'd managed to change their 'unchangeable ticket' to allow them to leave from Launceston."

Bob adds: *"For the record, Launceston's airport services several 737 arrivals and departures daily."*

Bob and Joy returned home from saying their farewells to find a large sign in the window of the downstairs apartment used by their guests, "Apartment for rent". Goodness knows what the neighbours thought.

But that wasn't the end of it. It seems the house is destined for the real estate market. *"When we were away on another exchange to Canada, we had permitted an elderly, retired minister and his wife from Queensland the use of our house and car before our Canadian exchange guests arrived.*

Our house guests noticed some activity on the front lawn one day where there was a bloke putting up a real estate "For Sale" sign. Absolutely certain that we had not given thought to selling our house, the minister went out and explained the situation.

The following day, the same guy appeared again and proceeded to place the sign on our vacant block next door. Again, the minister had to intervene and tell him to take his sign away."

Related Lodging Alternatives

*T*here are a number of lodging alternatives related to home exchange and which offer many of the same benefits. These are:

Hospitality exchange

Homestay

Unsynchronised exchange

House-sitting offered

House-sitter wanted

Rental available

Youth hospitality exchange

Non-reciprocal exchange

Consecutive exchange series

Transaction combination

HOSPITALITY EXCHANGE

Participants offer hospitality at their home in return for reciprocal hospitality at a later date. This is often taken up by single travellers and for shorter stays. Guests are generally treated as one of the family with meals offered by mutual arrangement.

Participants aren't likely to stay for long so even non-reciprocal short stays are easy to arrange. Host parties are often happy to take the plunge with people they don't know on the basis that the worst that they're likely to experience is a bore!

This is a great way to make international friends especially for seniors travelling alone who may enjoy the company of a local host in an unfamiliar country. It also allows the traveller some independence in moving around a country without the confines of a tour, crowded coaches or rigid itineraries.

Once the parties have met and determined that they get along amicably, the arrangement may result in a longer stay, extra meals, tours or other gestures. Tours of the local area and environs are usually included.

Robert from Napier, New Zealand travelling with his wife Helen to England, had this to say about hospitality exchanging:

"We have just returned from a two months trip to Britain where we had several hospitality exchanges as a result of our Latitudes Home Exchange membership and we very satisfied with the outcome. If we travel again, we will rejoin.

Hospitality exchanges solve the problem of both parties having to travel at the same time and allow people to move around quite a lot when travelling without committing to several weeks in one town.

Several of the people we contacted were interested in having us stay because they were planning to visit New Zealand some time in the next two years. In some cases they already had a firm date.

We asked to stay for two or three nights, and people seemed to be happy to take the plunge with people they didn't know on the basis that if it didn't work out, it wasn't a long time to have to put up with us. With non-simultaneous hosting, you aren't likely to stay anywhere for long. Short stays are so easy to arrange this way.

Another advantage is that when they do claim their return hospitality, they will be staying with people who have become their friends."

Hospitality exchange requires almost no planning. Because you are not trying to arrange travel dates which coincide with another party, it is a simple matter of ensuring that your dates are convenient to your potential hosts.

Usually a reciprocal offer would be extended to the same party who has hosted you, but in many cases you would ultimately host a third party in the spirit of 'what goes around comes around'.

Cynthia and Brian of Wanaka in New Zealand's South Island extended hospitality to a couple from Nova Scotia. Cynthia explains how it worked: *"We invited them to stay with us, agreeing to split the household bills such as weekly groceries. We lived like family, we ate together and drove them around the local environs. We weren't sure how it would work out but, as we have an extra upstairs sitting room, we thought that would give us some privacy if needed. It all worked out very well.*

We only have one car so we could only give them free use of it at weekends when they went off for weekend trips on their own. For part of their stay in New Zealand, I organised a train trip for them to travel north to Auckland and they rented a car for the remainder of their time.

They stayed with us for about two weeks of their total stay in New Zealand. We might go to Canada to take up the reciprocal offer but if we don't, it doesn't matter. We enjoyed having them stay."

It is imperative not to arrive unannounced; you must have prior confirmation from the hosts. An initial proposal offering hospitality exchange as a transaction means that the owners are willing to consider hosting guests as well as being hosted themselves. It does not serve as an open invitation for anyone to show up on their doorstep.

HOMESTAY

Homestay is a variation on hospitality exchange and is usually a non-reciprocal arrangement. The purpose is to promote understanding and cultural exchange between people of different countries.

Board and lodging is provided with an established host. The hospitality is not free but the costs are generally cheaper than hotels and you get a lot more for your money. A typical homestay would last two or three weeks but could be a month or longer. Homestays are generally arranged through organisations or sponsors specialising in such arrangements rather than the traditional home exchange clubs.

The organisation will generally undertake to select a family and location that suits your individual interests. Some organisations link your homestay with study courses, language classes or professional interests.

You will usually have a private room in the family home or a self-contained unit. In some cases, all meals will be provided but you can expect to receive breakfast and dinner.

UNSYNCHRONISED EXCHANGE

Where swappers own a second home, they may offer either their primary residence or the second home for exchange, enabling both parties to travel at their preferred times. This is useful in the case of exchanges between the two hemispheres where the seasonal variations may limit the scope of mutually acceptable exchange times.

Dick of New Jersey is fortunate to be able to use a second home to his advantage. *"I am in an exchange with a family from Carnlough, Northern Ireland. They are currently at my summer home in Surf City, New Jersey and Jean and I will be going to Ireland in September. In as much as both houses are summer homes, second houses, our exchange did not have to be simultaneous. Hence, we can almost act as host for each other's visit. It is working out well. If anyone wants testimony, just have them contact me."*

Some trust will be required on the part of the second party to travel since a period of time will pass before they get to avail themselves of the reciprocal offer. There exists the possibility that the home gets sold in the meantime.

Another aspect of second or holiday homes is that they are sometimes not as well equipped as a primary residence might be. If you are exchanging your primary residence for a second home, it would be wise to investigate exactly what is available.

If you need only a base from which to travel to other destinations, a second home may be ideal for your needs. For those seeking all the home comforts, you may find a second home lacking in such amenities as an extensive book library, VCR, full complement of cutlery and kitchen accessories.

Long-time exchangers, Rob and Betty of Perth filed this report after they'd exchanged their primary home for a second home in England: *"The house was really a holiday flat, very small and basic. It was comfortable and clean but lacking in comforts for a long stay. There were no drying facilities for winter washing; no rails, dryer or clothes airer.*

It had no toilet roll holder so we bought them one and installed it. There were no hooks or towel rails in the bathroom and the towels were threadbare. There were two tea towels and limited cutlery. The microwave was very small, no video or remote control for TV. There were no games, cards and just a few books. They'd put a bar on overseas calls which they hadn't mentioned."

Cynthia and Brian of Wanaka made use of a farm cottage in France which belonged to a British resident. Cynthia says: *"Although it was a holiday home, it was very comfortable. The owner, unfortunately, had a heart attack while travelling in South Africa and wasn't able to take up the reciprocal hospitality at the time but the offer remains open and we hope he might come to New Zealand in the future.*

Although he couldn't travel overseas himself, he was kind enough to take himself off somewhere during the one week we had scheduled to spend in his UK home. We spent one night with him there before he left."

HOUSE-SITTING OFFERED

Some home exchange clubs include details of people offering house-sitting services while there are other organisations dedicated exclusively to this type of transaction. Typically, they provide a registry of available house-sitters, homes available for house-sitting or both.

It is usually the house-sitter that pays any membership fees to the club. There are usually no fees for people seeking house-sitters.

House-sitters should be able to provide references and a police clearance on request. They should expect to make a financial contribution to utility and telephone bills and be willing to care for plants and pets as required by the owners.

People who are genuinely receptive to the concept of house exchange, but who have been unable to secure an exchange make the most grateful, responsible house-sitters.

HOUSE-SITTER WANTED

Travellers who have alternative accommodation organised at their destination sometimes make their home available to others for security purposes or out of a genuine desire to offer hospitality to overseas guests. The incoming guest handles mail, cares for plants and pets and may be expected to pay utility bills during their stay.

Margaret and Neil have a home in Australia and regularly take overseas trips. Home exchange wouldn't be practical as they tend to move around visiting family and friends in various countries. Instead, they make their home available to house-sitters in their absence. Margaret explains how it works:

"We find that, for short holidays, house-sitters suit us better than trying to find a tenant. We usually use a house-sitting club although once we found our sitter through a home exchange club. We contacted

various agencies and then selected one depending on the availability of their sitters and the costs involved. We expect to pay approximately AU$250 for a three week period.

The sitter is required to secure a 'police clearance' which means they have been checked out to eliminate any past misconduct or convictions on police records.

A representative from the house-sitting club comes to check over the home and animals and completes some paperwork. Some agencies take videos of the home contents, garden and swimming pool to document the status prior to the house-sitter's occupation.

There is very little preparation required. The club puts the house-sitter in touch with us and we arrange a meeting to discuss what is required of them concerning care of animals, plants, pool, garden, etc.

The sitter is expected to buy their own food and pay for their own telephone calls. We pay for the gas and electricity during their stay although some agencies recommend that the sitter pay a percentage of the bill.

We designate a close friend or family member who can make major decisions on our behalf while we're away.

There is always an element of risk having a complete stranger look after one's home and pets. We try to find someone who is used to dealing with animals and who doesn't object to walking our dog three or four times a week. We have found our sitters to be exceptionally good.

When we went to Europe for a month, we had a couple from the USA who planted new plants in the garden, tidied and cleaned our shed and left us flowers for our return. In this particular case, we had allowed them use of our vehicle as well. They had looked after it alright but some weeks after their return, we received a speeding ticket in the mail. We were able to satisfy the authorities that we'd been out of the country and we didn't have to pay it."

RENTAL AVAILABLE

Where a home exchange is genuinely unattainable, some clubs allow their members to offer their home for rent. This is not intended as a means of capitalising on excessive rents from unsuspecting overseas visitors. Instead any monies received can be used to offset the owner's own accommodation expenses abroad.

Commercial properties should be avoided and the home owner should be genuinely receptive to the concept of home exchange. The rental amount should be kept to a minimum to ensure the relationship remains one of mutual trust, rather than that of landlord/tenant.

YOUTH HOSPITALITY EXCHANGE

A teenager, often the offspring of a home swap club member, stays with a host family overseas in return for reciprocal hospitality for the teenager of that family. This is an ideal way for young people to learn a language, discover a new culture and to promote understanding between people of different countries.

NON-RECIPROCAL EXCHANGES

Sometimes it seems no-one at your destination choice wants to come to your location when you wish to travel. At *Latitudes Home Exchange,* we found that at peak travel times such as during the Christmas or Easter holidays, many families were requesting similar travel dates but their destinations didn't match. We decided to offer these members what we called 'three-way exchanges'.

The first to undertake a three-way exchange involved each of the three couples (from Perth, Hobart and Sydney respectively) moving 'one state to the left' within Australia in order to attain the exchange destination they wanted.

We realised that the reciprocity and mutual caring normally inherent in a two-party exchange would not apply since each party would occupy the home of a second party, with a third party making use of their own home. Because the couples were well-matched and like-minded, this did not present a problem as Sid and Maureen, the Sydney couple, explain:

"I should just like to add a few comments to our follow up report. We can't believe how smoothly everything went and here we are safely back after a wonderful holiday wondering why we didn't do an exchange years ago.

As you know we met Ken and Chris briefly in Hobart before they flew off to Perth and, on our return, Rob and Betty met us at Sydney airport before flying back to Perth. Both couples were really nice people and we wish we could have spent more time with them. Rob and Betty left our home and car in perfect order – I am sure it was cleaner than I'd left it – and this experience has made us even keener to get going again.

This exchange worked out very well. It gave us a holiday that we could not otherwise have afforded with accommodation costs. It was really home from home, far better than the cold atmosphere of a hotel.

We have spoken to many of our friends about home exchanges and once they get over the 'I couldn't have strangers living in my home' they can see how enthusiastic we are and what a great idea it is. Our next door neighbour is particularly interested so expect a call from No. 6."

Of course, with three couples involved, it did involve a little more correspondence and planning than would be necessary for a standard two-party exchange but all agreed it was worth it. Ken and Chris from Tasmania reported:

"The three way switch was very successful through good communication by letter and phone – but this should be carried out for all exchanges. We enjoyed our exchange and appeared to have similar ways of living; enjoying house and garden. On our return, we found everything clean and tidy."

Settlement of bills was carried out as usual and mutual respect was extended to all concerned. Rob and Betty, the third couple involved said, *"We were very happy indeed with the whole set-up. We were all well-matched and having the dates synchronised by our club made all the difference. Both car and property were left in excellent condition.*

Money was left to cover telephone bills and other accounts were settled as agreed. We exchanged letters and calls with both couples and met the daughter of the Hobart couple who lives here in Perth. We recommend these arrangements to all exchangers."

CONSECUTIVE EXCHANGE SERIES

Some people use home exchange to cover all or part of an extensive itinerary involving several destinations. They might stay in several different towns in one country or arrange an exchange in several countries.

With advance planning, the number of nights requiring interim accommodation can be considerably reduced. Inevitably though, it would be necessary to plan for some hotel or B&B expenses in between the home exchanges.

If you arrange such a holiday, you'll need a back-up plan should one part of the chain fall apart. You won't want to find yourselves paying for hotel accommodation for several weeks or months while you await the next leg of your trip. Remember, you will still have a responsibility to the other parties in the series who won't want to be let down by your changing plans.

If you're swapping with a family for whom you form one part of a series of exchanges, make sure they confirm that the exchange with your family will still go ahead in the event of one part of the chain collapsing.

When Ken and June of London were unable to find a party prepared to spend three months in England during the peak winter months, they agreed to let their club arrange a series of three consecutive exchanges within Australia. This arrangement not only afforded them the opportunity to escape the dreary British winter but they were able to experience life in three very different parts of Australia.

Consecutive exchanges can also be used for more than one stay in the same town where it has not been possible to find a party prepared to exchange for the required length of stay. Instead of swapping for a period of four months, for example, a family might agree to accept two consecutive exchanges in the same town which, together, cover the desired four month period. It must be stressed that such arrangements require much advance planning and a great deal of correspondence. Consequently, there are few, if any, formal clubs willing to undertake such a brief.

It is more likely that you'll be putting these plans together yourself. Usually this will be organised from information provided by a formal club such as a printed or electronic directory of members. These procedures are covered in detail in the chapter entitled, *Getting Started*.

In 1998, retirees Frank and Sandy of Eagle Heights, Queensland successfully put together a six month overseas trip involving five home exchanges in four different countries. In the

UK, they swapped in Cornwall and Cambridge. The other three exchange homes were located in Kessel, Belgium; Tilburg, Holland and Nerja, Spain.

From these bases, they were able to visit Wales, Scotland, Luxembourg and Morocco. On the outbound journey, they visited China for ten days and on the return trip they stopped in New York for one week. They say they accomplished all this for little more than the cost of the airfares.

TRANSACTION COMBINATION

Some people use a combination of transactions to achieve a desired itinerary. This may comprise a house exchange for use as a base on arrival, the use of B&B accommodation for a few extra nights and perhaps some hospitality exchanges along the way.

How the Internet has Revolutionised Home Swapping

*R*elying on the traditional postal service, home swap participants would typically send off a large package of information containing photographs, letter of introduction, details about the home on offer and maybe some tourist brochures as bait.

The package might take several days or weeks to arrive at its destination and, assuming the recipient replied in a timely manner, the same length of time to receive the answer. If this process was repeated twenty or thirty times, the expense would not be insignificant when we consider the costs associated with airmail postage of bulky materials.

Let's assume conservatively that a month has now passed. No reply has yet been received from the party of first choice. But positive answers have now been received from two or three of the less appealing offers. Should these people be kept waiting in the hope of hearing from the preferred party? This strategy could risk missing out altogether!

Each offer could, of course, be briefly acknowledged without making any firm commitment. If one of these offers is firmly accepted, it will no longer be possible to pursue the property of choice.

So much time has now passed that, with many people all 'hedging their bets' for their preferred choice, it is inevitable that some, if not all, of them will be quite disappointed.

Enter email. Home exchange is a prime example of the way technology has revolutionised our lives. The internet lends itself very well to the home swapping process. It affords instant communication between swapping hopefuls. We can now send a very brief message asking another home swapper whether there is any interest in our area at a proposed time.

The message is relayed to the recipient almost instantaneously and is available as soon as he or she next logs on to the internet. This abolishes all the inconveniences normally associated with communication over several time zones.

At the click of a 'Reply' button, the answer is sent immediately, freeing the enquirer to pursue other options or inviting him to send more details. The whole deal can be potentially clinched within 24 hours! No-one need be disappointed.

People are more likely to reply since the process is literally as simple as clicking a button, and for just the cost of a local call.

It could be argued that fax machines provide a similar service, although the costs associated are greater since the sender must pay the cost of the international call for the duration of the transmission and for each message sent. Then there are the time zone problems to overcome, choosing a time that is 'off-peak' for the sender but which won't inconvenience the recipient.

I couldn't count the number of people I have woken from a deep sleep, sending them downstairs in their pyjamas to switch on the computer in the middle of the night followed by the long silence while we both wait for the computer to boot up and the sleepy, irritated owner initialises his fax modem. That can really get you off to a bad start. All because I'd incorrectly assumed they would have a dedicated line for their fax machine.

One couple in the their seventies, Fred and Ivy, immediately realised the value of the internet on joining the printed directory service. Viewing so many entries with email addresses, they knew they would miss out if they didn't have email facilities.

Never having even turned on a computer before, they purchased one, got an internet connection and took some introductory computing classes at the local Adult Education Centre. Within weeks, Fred was calling me to boast of their consecutive exchanges planned for France, Germany and Switzerland for the upcoming summer.

Using a scanner, a relatively inexpensive accessory, and the necessary software to view the images, photographs can be readily exchanged via the internet. It is important to scan photos at a low resolution (no greater than 100 dpi or dots per inch) for transmission because large files take a long time to transmit which will frustrate you as well as the recipient.

The most readily accepted file format for internet use is the JPEG (.jpg) format. JPEG stands for Joint Photographic Experts Group and is an image format that is supported by most web browsers. Because it can display an unlimited number of colours and its compression routine is optimised for photographs, jpg is well suited to sending and displaying photographic images on the web.

The internet has also facilitated the speed at which full service agencies can arrange exchanges for their members. It lends itself perfectly to this application and has made these companies very efficient.

It has also led to many new start-up companies springing up, hoping to take full advantage of the technology. Choosing a reputable home exchange company that is suitable for your needs is discussed in the chapter entitled, *Getting Started.*

Getting Started

PLANNING AHEAD

*S*tart organising your home exchange as soon as your travel plans are known. Approximately six months advance planning would be ideal but there's nothing to lose by starting even earlier. If you're joining a formal club, the earlier you join, the more contacts you stand to make. If you joined one year in advance, the worst that could happen is that you don't find anyone to swap with and end up paying an additional membership fee – better than missing out altogether.

Another good reason to plan ahead is that many of the members you contact might have other plans for the upcoming year but may well consider your offer in a subsequent year. This is particularly true of exchanges involving destinations separated by many travel miles.

DECIDING WHETHER TO REGISTER WITH A FORMAL HOME EXCHANGE CLUB

There are a number of ways that you can arrange an exchange. The ideal way is to swap with someone you already know such as a friend or family member. Other options include advertising independently or publishing your own web site. Alternatively, you may choose to go through a formal home swapping organisation.

FRIENDS AND FAMILY

You might know of someone through your own network of friends and contacts that would enjoy coming to your destination at the same time that you're planning your own trip. Perhaps you have family members who would like to take advantage of this type of arrangement. Ask your friends to put the word out on your behalf and you might just be fortunate enough to be able to make a suitable arrangement with someone you know or through mutual friends.

ADVERTISING

If you don't know of anyone who would be suitable for a private arrangement, you can consider advertising.

If you have a very specific destination in mind, you should advertise in the local area. This can be done by taking out a classified advert in a community or regional paper in the locale of your intended destination.

Alternatively, you can ask friends or relatives at the destination to place adverts in newsagents and places of communal gathering. If they are prepared to provide their local phone number and to field enquiries on your behalf, this is likely to generate a higher response than if the respondent must call overseas or long distance. This localised approach can, however, prove extremely limiting.

National newspapers can be used if your plans are less specific. Keep in mind that, in taking this approach, you have to pay for the privilege of advertising to the population at large, the vast majority of whom will not be a candidate for a home exchange with you.

It is therefore not very cost-effective and you may find that, for less than the cost of an advert placed for only one day in one of the major papers, you could have funded your annual membership with one of the formal home exchange clubs.

PUBLISHING A PERSONAL WEB SITE

With some basic computing skills, it is possible to publish to your own home page which can advertise your home exchange proposal. You are able to show with the aid of colour photographs what you have on offer and state what you are seeking.

You need a scanner, File Transfer Protocol (FTP) program software such as WS_FTP or CuteFTP and an internet connection. Many Internet Service Providers (ISPs) provide ample space to host a personal home page as part of the internet package.

There are software programs available to convert your text into Hyper Text Markup Language (HTML) so it is no longer necessary to know how to author a web page. Information on web site authoring and publishing is freely available in tutorial form on the internet.

Your ISP should provide all the basic information you require to publish and upload your web site but it is unlikely that they will offer free support if you need assistance in its creation and development.

This approach would be suitable for career-swappers, that is, people who are open to the on-going possibilities that home swapping might bring. It is also suitable for people who use formal clubs as the web site can provide an inexpensive showcase of what you have available to interested parties. Details, dates and destinations can be changed and upgraded instantly. Testimonials can be added.

Publishing a personal home page would be less effective for a single, specific exchange proposal unless ample time is allowed between publishing the site and the departure date.

You need to have a good understanding of how to promote your web site including the value of metatags and how to submit your site to the search engines for proper cataloguing. It is probably necessary to use some form of paid advertising to drive traffic to your web site.

Although potentially available to millions of users, unless your site is properly indexed, the chances of even one person stumbling upon it are extremely remote. Without knowing your web site address (URL), it would be like finding a needle in a haystack.

FORMAL CLUBS

Formal clubs do all the groundwork for you. Through their extensive marketing efforts, they gather the information and compile a comprehensive catalogue of members.

Everyone listed in these catalogues has been pre-qualified as being interested in the concept of home swapping. So you are left only with the task of identifying those suitable to your particular needs and narrowing those options down to one party.

Of the estimated 200,000 people who swap their homes each year, only a minute fraction are arranged outside the networks of formal clubs.

There are basically two types of clubs. One is the catalogue-based club whose sole function is to compile a registry of its members and distribute that information to subscribed members. It may distribute printed catalogues or provide the information by electronic means such as through a web site or on CD ROM.

The other is the full service club which seeks to match its members by specific criteria. Typically, you do not have access to the full database. Instead you are sent the details of a single proposed exchange property for your perusal.

Finally, there are a few clubs which offer their members a choice of services.

The following explains the three most common service options, what they cost, how they work and the advantages and disadvantages of each. They are internet listing, printed directory publication and custom matching services.

1. Internet listing

What is it?

An internet listing is one whereby your home details are published on the web site of a home exchange club on the World Wide Web. In recent years, there have been many start-up home exchange companies offering such a service.

"We just wanted you to know what a great response we've had. Of all the members we contacted, only two people haven't replied. We're leaving for Wales in October and the owners have already arranged for their neighbours to pick us up at Manchester airport! We are really excited about our first exchange."

John and Fran W., Perth, Western Australia

"Your service works! I joined up only two days ago and yesterday we secured an exchange to England. I think your members in West Sussex were as surprised as we were!"

Nan McM., Perth, Western Australia

How does it work?

Firstly, you'll need the web site address (URL) of the company. It will look something like this: **http://www.home-swap.com**

If you don't know the web site address, you can find many companies by using a search engine and entering keywords such as 'homeswap'. Once you've found the web site, you will be able to complete an on-line application form.

Here, you are required to provide information concerning your travelling party, your home and your environs. Some or all of this information is displayed in the form of a listing.

Depending on the club and its regard for your privacy, this information may be made available to the internet world at large or it may be restricted to its paid members. Alternatively, the club may allow non-members to contact you by email while masking your identity and concealing your email address.

You are typically given the opportunity to submit at least one photograph to enhance your listing which can attract an additional fee. Take advantage of this option because photos appear in colour and can provide a far greater sense of what is on offer than a text-only listing. 'A picture speaks a thousand words' definitely holds true in this application.

If you have a scanner, it is possible to scan and upload a photo yourself. The club will advise on the specifications for photo submission to their particular web site. Expect to be required to provide your photos in a .jpg file format.

Clubs providing a reasonable level of service allow you to send in a photograph via the postal mail which they can scan and upload to your listing for you.

In most cases, you are expected to make your payment on-line using your credit card. If this is the only payment accepted and you are prepared to make the payment on-line, make sure that the site is secure. You can easily check this in your browser where you will find a closed padlock for Netscape and a lock icon on Internet Explorer displayed on the status bar.

Note that not all the pages of the web site need be secure – only those pages where you are transferring information, that is, either your credit card details or your personal information.

If the site is not secure and there are no alternative payment options, find another company. If they have no regard for the security of your private details, they do not deserve your business. This applies to all on-line trading, not just home swapping clubs.

Once you've submitted your application and membership fees, you should hear from the club right away providing you with a username and password which gives you access to the complete database.

You may receive some helpful tips in the form of an automatic email but, generally speaking, from now on you'll be on your own in terms of finding a suitable exchange party.

Before you join an internet-based home exchange club, it might pay to enquire of them what form their guidelines take (assuming any are provided) and what level of support they can provide.

You'll also want to know how their search engine works because you will spend a good deal of your time searching for suitable properties. Ideally, it will allow non-members to conduct a search of all the properties while protecting the identity and privacy of its members.

This means that, before you join, you would have access to the full scope of properties but without the member's name or contact details. In other words, you need to become a member before you are able to make contact with other members.

Some home exchange club web sites allow you to search only by country. Others require that you enter very specific details surrounding place and date.

On the best sites, you can search by any criteria you desire such as destination country, specific town, number of bedrooms, smoking status and even by members wishing to come to *your* area.

Figure 3 shows a typical home listing on *Latitudes Home Exchange* web site.

Figure 3. Sample Web Site Listing

Maidenhead, GREAT BRITAIN ENGLAND

Most members joining via the internet have access to email facilities and therefore it is safe to assume that you'll be able to contact most other on-line members via email.

The club's listings should have an email hyperlink facility. This means that, when you click on the email address shown within a particular listing, that email address is automatically pasted directly into your email server in readiness for you to send the email expressing your initial interest.

Most on-line memberships are valid for a twelve month period. During that time, you should have full access to your own listing so that you can make amendments whenever you desire. In fact, you should be encouraged to do so, because sifting through expired or fulfilled requests is frustrating and time-consuming for new members.

Advantages

✓ This is the most cost-effective service option. Clubs can offer reasonably priced memberships because they have little or no involvement in the process of finding your exchange.

✓ Email facilities afford the most timely responses from other members.

✓ Because of the ease and lack of expense in replying, you are likely to receive some form of response even if only to decline your offer.

✓ Listings are generally up to date (provided the individual members have the means and motivation to attend to this).

Disadvantages

✗ Using the internet, there are the inevitable privacy issues. The site may be secure but all it takes is one unsavoury person or company prepared to pay the membership fee to compromise that security.

✗ Web sites are prime targets for piracy and plagiarism from start-up clubs and those with no business acumen of their own. You could find your listing on the open web sites of other clubs.

✗ Even if the site is secure, you run the risk of unscrupulous operators infiltrating the database with the intention of compiling email address lists or other lists which utilise your personal information.

What does it cost?

Some internet companies offer free membership, usually while they are building their property database. Others ask for a small donation should you feel their site proved of value to you. The average cost for a twelve month on-line membership is US$30 with those at the higher end of the scale being around US$95.

2. Printed Directory Publication

What is it?

During the course of a membership year, subscribers to a printed directory publication service will receive a number of catalogues, or printed directories, containing the listings of other current subscribers around the world.

"It cost $100 to join the directory service and we had more than a hundred dollars worth of excitement before we went anywhere, just reading the directories and dreaming about the possibilities."

Pat C., Bathurst, New South Wales

"Although we are all settled with our exchange plans, we are still looking forward to the next directory edition, it makes exciting reading thinking of all the possibilities for next time."

Penny B., Sydney, New South Wales

How does it work?

A membership fee, usually payable on an annual and renewable basis, entitles you to list your property in one or more of a series of printed directories which are distributed throughout an international membership network.

The number and frequency of directories received depends on the individual club. You may receive only one catalogue for your membership fee with future editions available as required for an extra fee or you may receive up to five printed editions distributed throughout the year.

The rationale behind the timing of release dates of some publications is somewhat of a mystery with some clubs having lengthy 'dry spells' between publications followed by a seemingly rapid succession of editions. Therefore, you'll need to time your application carefully to ensure inclusion in an edition that allows adequate planning time for your intended trip.

You may have the option to provide one photograph of your home to appear with your listing, usually for an additional fee. This is generally worth the extra money because it gives other members browsing through the directory a better idea of what is on offer.

Your photo may appear in colour or black and white. One clear view of the exterior is generally the best option if you live in a house. If yours is a flat or apartment, a shot of the main living area is sufficient. For people boasting excellent views, a photo of the view can be used. The club will advise of any specific requirements.

Once you receive the catalogue of members, you start to identify those which appeal to your family. The club you join should provide you with a set of guidelines describing how to go about contacting other members.

They should also explain how much detail to provide to prospective swappers and at what stage that information should be provided. In the meantime, you receive expressions of interest from members who have seen your listing.

Table 3 shows a property listing which you might expect to find in a printed directory.

Table 3. Sample printed directory listing

		EUROPE	BELGIUM
Gudrun ********	***** ** ** ** (hm)		VILLERS-LA-VILLE
********	***** ** ** **(wk)	6 persons	Brussels - 40km
Villers-la-Ville	Gudrun@******	hmx	house, 160sm, 4bd/1ba
Belgium			

3ad/4ch(8,6,1,0)
Engineer/Dance teacher, non-smokers

Nice family home (3-storey, modern kitchen, fireplace, bathroom with jacuzzi, 3 toilets) with big quiet garden, in a small but interesting village in the heart of Belgium and Europe. For those who like to travel: Paris, London, Amsterdam, Cologne and the North Sea are only 2-3 hr ride (possible daytrip). For children: house and garden fully equipped and attraction parks with tropic pool are only 10 km far. 5 bicycles available, golf place, horse stables, ultra light airport etc. within 10 km. Big forest 5 min walk. Famous abbey, old castles and a lot of other historic places are not far (Waterloo, Brussels, Brugge etc.). We have a cat, some birds and an aquarium and are looking forward to making our first exchange experience. Central heating, usual appliances, washing machine/ dryer, phone, garage, local shops/restaurants, sea/beach, fishing, sailing, golf, horse riding, bicycles, baby-sitting. All facilities for babies. Train station 5 min walk. Lake for surfing/sailing 30 min ride. Lots of tourist attractions not far: see old monasteries, castles, flea market every Saturday, etc. We search for a home near a lake or beach, if not, then a swimming pool. Car exchange. No smokers.

SOUTH EUROPE, MOROCCO, open to offers
max 4 wks   school holidays, flexible   LT-002-BE-9100-p

Somewhere in the directory, there should be a key to the listings as well as clear interpretation of any codes and abbreviations (see Table 4).

Table 4. Sample key to directory listings

Note: mailing address may be different from the exchange address

name(s) and mailing address	tel/fax/email contact details	accommodates transaction(s)	distance to nearest large town listing location
Gudrun ******** ******** Villers-la-Ville Belgium	***** ** ** ** (hm) ***** ** ** **(wk) Gudrun@******	6 persons hmx	VILLERS-LA-VILLE Brussels - 40km house, 160sm, 4bd/1ba

accomm. type and size

3ad/4ch(8,6,1,0) —— *persons travelling*

Engineer/Dance teacher, non-smokers —— *travelling party profile*

Nice family home (3-storey, modern kitchen, fireplace, bathroom with jacuzzi, 3 toilets) with big quiet garden, in a small but interesting village in the heart of Belgium and Europe. For those who like to travel: Paris, London, Amsterdam, Cologne and the North Sea are only 2-3 hr ride (possible daytrip). For children: house and garden fully equipped and attraction parks with tropic pool are only 10 km far. 5 bicycles available, golf place, horse stables, ultra light airport etc. within 10 km. Big forest 5 min walk. Famous abbey, old castles and a lot of other historic places are not far (Waterloo, Brussels, Brugge etc.). We have a cat, some birds and an aquarium and are looking forward to making our first exchange experience. Central heating, usual appliances, washing machine/dryer, phone, garage, local shops/restaurants, sea/beach, fishing, sailing, golf, horse riding, bicycles, baby-sitting. All facilities for babies. Train station 5 min walk. Lake for surfing/sailing 30 min ride. Lots of tourist attractions not far: see old monasteries, castles, flea market every Saturday, etc. We search for a home near a lake or beach, if not, then a swimming pool. Car exchange. No smokers.

SOUTH EUROPE, MOROCCO, open to offers

max 4 wks   school holidays, flexible   LT-002-BE-9100-p

preferred length of stay   *preferred dates*   *preferred destination(s)*   *member ref. number*

ABBREVIATIONS

For ease of reading, we have attempted to limit the use of abbreviations. To assist members for whom English is a second language, you may see some commonly used terms abbreviated as explained below.

flexible	duration and dates flexible	for/mtn	forests/mountains
a/c	air-conditioning	fp	fireplace
ad,ch,tn	adult, children, teenagers	gge	garage
adq transport	adequate public transport	lib	public library
ba	bathrooms	pkg	off-street parking
bd	bedrooms	pet care o/d	pet care offered/desired
cd	compact disc player	pks/plgrnd	parks/playground
ch	central heating	pool (pub)	public swimming pool
car recom/nec	car recommended/necessary	pool (pvt)	private swimming pool
exp exch	experienced exchangers	very quiet	the neighbourhood

TRANSACTIONS

hmx	home exchange	ro	rental available
hpx	hospitality home exchange	yhx	youth hospitality exchange
uns	unsynchronised exchange	wkx	weekend exchange/short break
hso	house-sitting offered	o, open	open to offers
hsw	house-sitter wanted		

Some clubs allow private listings or unlisted memberships. A *private listing* means that you may list your home without having your name or contact details printed. Instead, the contact address, telephone, email and fax details of the home exchange club are given and the club forwards to you any correspondence from other members.

An *unlisted membership* is one where access to the printed catalogues is granted but where the member's own details are omitted. A home exchange club owner should perhaps be wary of a party purporting to be interested in the home exchange concept yet sufficiently untrusting of other members as to avoid making their own details available to them.

Advantages

✓ All of the properties currently available since the last publication are indexed and sorted by country, enabling ease of reading and searching.

✓ The selection of exchange opportunities is considerably greater than through a custom matching service.

✓ Provides the opportunity to advertise your exchange proposal to those people who do not have internet access.

✓ Once the initial preparation of fact sheets about your family, home and area have been completed for the first exchange, procedures for subsequent exchanges are easy.

✓ Provides many contacts from which you can arrange multiple exchanges or exchanges in subsequent years.

Disadvantages

✗ As a first-time exchanger, it can be time-consuming preparing the initial fact and information sheets.

✗ Not as cost-effective as internet services because you need to factor in the cost of international postage stamps or fax calls and stationery.

✗ Because of the costs associated with traditional mail and faxing, many members choose not to reply to all enquiries made of them. This can be frustrating to those taking an active approach.

✗ Members living in highly sought-after areas will receive dozens of requests. It is not always practical for them to reply to each of these.

✗ The person to whom you've written may be away on an extended exchange when your proposal arrives. This can cause lengthy delays in getting a reply.

✗ Many clubs post their new listings on their web sites as received. Subscribers to printed directories who do not have access to email facilities may find that many listings have already been snapped up by the time of publication.

✗ Some club listings contain many abbreviations and coding which can be frustrating to wade through.

What does it cost?

Annual subscriptions vary from US$57 to US$137. Many clubs now offer on-line access to their listings at no extra cost.

3.   Custom matching

What is it?

As the name implies, custom matching is a service whereby the home exchange club attempts to find a suitable exchange party on your behalf. There are very few companies offering this level of service.

"Just writing to let you know we have arrived back home after a wonderful two months in Canada. Everything was beautifully arranged

when we arrived in Guelph. We feel we have had the trip of a lifetime and made very special friends. On arriving home, everything was perfect so, once again, many thanks for finding such a wonderful couple. I am sure we will be seeking your assistance for future exchanges."

Cecil and Joan E., Caloundra, Queensland

"I have told anyone who will listen to me all about your very professional service. A real personal touch all the way through. It was an absolute pleasure doing business with you. I am really impressed. You'll hear from us next year for sure. From now on we will only exchange for our holidays."

Martin and Fiona W., Perth, Western Australia

How does it work?

You are required to complete an application form, providing the necessary details to allow the particular club to carry out the task of finding a suitable match for you.

The extent and nature of the information required varies from club to club but you can expect to provide more details than for do-it-yourself service options.

Some clubs have a simple checklist while others require you to submit maps, brochures and photographs to make your offer more appealing.

Supporting documents may also be required such as character references, police clearance reports and a letter of introduction describing your travelling party. You are almost certainly expected to supply photographs of your house showing exterior and interior views as well as one of your travelling family.

Finally, you specify what you require in terms of the exchange home, your destination and date preferences. You should be given an opportunity to specify whether or not you accept smokers, small children and pets and any other restrictions you wish to impose.

Once you have gathered the necessary information, it is sent to your club of choice along with a registration fee for processing your application.

The club will now process your application and set about finding you a suitable exchange party. How they go about this is determined by their own procedures. Some clubs claim to have a 'computerised matching service' which is nothing more than scanning their existing databases for likely prospects, the details of which are forwarded to you. From then on, you're on your own.

Other clubs forward your summary information package to their agents in your destination country. The agent conducts a search of his own listings for a suitable match. The details of that proposed match are forwarded to the 'host agent' (through which you joined). At the same time, your details are forwarded to his own member for approval.

Still others forward your information to their affiliate clubs in your destination country. This is the way in which several smaller agencies in Europe operate.

Typically, you then receive a package, similar to the one you submitted yourself, detailing a proposed exchange family and property. You have all the information on which to base your decision but you are not provided with the name or contact details of the other party at this stage.

You may have questions about the proposed property and its owners and there may follow a period of 'negotiation' between the host agents on behalf of the two parties concerned. This may include such issues as approximate timeframes, acceptance of young children or other factors requiring flexibility on the part of one or both parties in order to make the exchange details equitable.

Once both parties are satisfied with the arrangements, you are expected to formally accept the proposed exchange home.

You are now entering into a contract with the home exchange club rather than with the other party. This may involve signing a contract of some description and will certainly require the submission of a fee.

Contracts are intended to be legally binding but, in reality, are little more than a good faith gesture on the part of the participating parties. You will probably be agreeing to something similar to that used at *Latitudes Home Exchange* (see Table 5).

Table 5. Sample Custom Matching Service Contract

> **LATITUDES HOME EXCHANGE CONTRACT**
> *Custom matching service*
>
> I/We _____ approve the exchange home reference _____ .
>
> I/We have received and read a copy of the *Latitudes Home Exchange* publication, 'Guidelines for a Successful Exchange' and understand my/ our obligations in accepting this exchange proposal.
>
> I/We agree to care for the exchange home in a responsible manner, maintain the property in the state in which it is found and report any damage, breakage or system failure to the designated person.
>
> I/We authorise *Latitudes Home Exchange* to release my/our name(s) to my/our proposed exchange partner(s) and understand that no contact details will be released under any circumstances until both parties have signed and returned their exchange contract and submitted the exchange fees.
>
> I/We understand that the exchange fees are submitted as confirmation of my/our intention to proceed with the exchange within the proposed timeframe and are non-refundable except in the unforeseen circumstance where the other party is forced to cancel due to death or illness and where *Latitudes Home Exchange* is unable to offer a suitable alternative.
>
> I/We understand that the function of *Latitudes Home Exchange* is to facilitate an introduction and that all further negotiations, including the finalisation of dates, are the responsibility of the parties involved.
>
> Signed _____ Date _____
>
> Signed _____ Date _____
>
> ©Latitudes Home Exchange 1993

Once both parties have made a commitment to their respective club, the contact details are released. If your club has a co-operative agreement with the club that your new exchange partners joined, it would be wise to investigate what instructions (if any) that club issues to its members. In particular, make sure they have a copy of the guidelines supplied by your own club so that both parties understand where the other is coming from with regard to the negotiations.

Advantages

✓ The club has greater control over the behaviour and movements of its members which deters members from behaving badly.

✓ Clubs offering custom matching services tend to have high customer loyalty due to the rapport gained through frequent communication.

✓ The club is likely to have references and reports on file from their members' previous exchange partners.

✓ Custom matching is far less time consuming for you than any other form of service available.

Disadvantages

✗ The club is carrying out all the groundwork on your behalf involving a great deal of correspondence so this service is more expensive than the do-it-yourself options.

✗ Clubs offering solely a custom matching service typically have less members and narrow geographical scope.

✗ You will not be offered a range of properties from which to choose. Typically, only one property is offered to you at a time which you will need to accept or decline before the next property is offered.

✗ If you continually reject proposals made to you, the club may grow weary of your inflexibility and the better offers will be made to more pliable members. This could result in your missing out altogether.

✗ If your stated criteria are too specific, in terms of destination, dates, acceptance of children and so on, the success rate could be lower because it will be hard for the club to find an exact match. They will not know that you might, perhaps, have considered other options had they been presented.

With flexibility being the key to successful home swapping, you might see an almost perfect offer in a large database and decide that you are prepared to bend your original rules somewhat. Therefore, the ability to view all available options, such as is possible through a printed or electronic directory, could increase your overall chances – provided you are flexible, of course.

What does it cost?

The fees for custom matching services are often broken down into two components. The first is a registration fee to cover the processing of your application and the second is a matching fee payable once a suitable exchange party has been secured.

Some clubs do not make any charges to register your application. Most clubs charge a nominal registration fee. This may be a one-time fee with future changes being made at no additional cost or it may represent an annual fee. Of those charging an annual registration fee, most carry this fee over to subsequent years if they are unable to match your initial request. The cost of the registration fee ranges from US$0-59.

Keep in mind that there is considerable work carried out by the club on your behalf before your proposal can be presented to its other members or to members of its affiliate clubs. In some cases, this may also involve translation of your application into another language. There are further costs associated with the presentation of your offer. These clubs are justified in requiring a nominal fee as a means of confirming your level of commitment as well as covering their administrative costs.

The second component is the matching fee. This is usually payable when both parties have confirmed the suitability of the proposed exchange partnership but before the contact details of the involved parties are revealed. This fee ranges from US$38-250.

FINDING THE RIGHT HOME EXCHANGE CLUB

"We have found a perfect exchange with a young couple and their three children in Brooklyn. We have all made our arrangements already and we all appear to be very pleased with the set-up. I was going to alert you shortly after we made the arrangements in late December but we were so busy with the end of the year preparations.

We are very pleased and have already highly recommended your exchange organization to several other people. If you ever need a pleased customer to give a testimonial, we are the candidates! Thanks again."

Carl and Mary H., Delta, British Columbia, Canada

With so many home exchange clubs to choose from, how do you make the right choice?

The ideal kind of recommendation comes from someone you know that can advocate a particular club. The choice may be narrowed if you have a specific service option in mind. Or, if you have a specific destination in mind, it could pay to join a small club based in that country since a club's geographic membership will typically be strongest in its home base.

To help you get started, you will find a list of home exchange companies at the end of this book. However, you are encouraged to research the various clubs yourself before making a commitment.

Selecting a club on-line

If you are selecting a club via the internet, it might pay to consider these points:

- Is the web site clearly set out and easy to navigate?

- Is the information well written or is it fraught with typos and poor grammar? The care with which the site has been developed could be a reflection of the overall state of the business.

- Are the answers to your questions readily available on the site?

- Can you find details of how to contact a live person via telephone, facsimile and snail mail?

- Is there is a contact name and a 'place of business' address?

- Are there local contacts in your country in case you have a difficulty after joining?

- Is there an email 'contact us' link clearly displayed?

- When you use that link, how quickly do you get a response?

- Does the response adequately address your specific questions or is it an automated reply that only vaguely meets your needs?

- Does the company invite comments and feedback from its users?

- When you read about the company, do you get a good feel for it and the people behind it?

- Does the site allow non-members to conduct a limited search of its properties while protecting the privacy of its members?

- Does the site provide any *verifiable* testimonials from its users? Is the club willing to put you in touch with these people?

- Does the company make it easy for you to make and pay for a transaction with them?

- Are there alternative payment options for people who do not wish to make a credit card payment over the internet?

- If you do wish to make a credit card payment, are your details protected by Secure Socket Layer transactions (SSL)?

- Does the company have a Privacy Statement?

- When was the web site last updated?

- Do they have a webmaster to handle technical questions?

- How will your contact details be displayed on the web site? Remember that 'open listings' are not only available to potential exchangers but to every junk email sender on the internet. Do you really want your name, address and phone numbers freely available to the world at large?

- What services do they offer? Make sure you find a company that offers the level of service with which you will be comfortable.

- What are the relative costs for the service? Remember there is no free lunch so if the service sounds too good to be true, it probably is. Start-up companies will often offer free listings while they build a database of members. This may be acceptable to you if other aspects of the company are equitable as everyone has to start somewhere. But don't expect to find a large selection of members available for exchanging. Watch out for free services in general because they may have a hidden agenda for your personal contact details such as compiling mailing lists for forward-selling to unscrupulous companies.

- How long have they been in operation? Keep in mind that many start-up home swapping companies have sprung up on the internet in recent years. And just as quickly, many of them have disappeared. Beware of parting with money if you don't get an overall impression that the company is committed to making their business succeed (i.e. investment in SSL).

- Does the membership database reflect the length of time in business? In other words, do they appear to have a commitment to expansion and growth or have they stagnated over the years?

- To what extent does the company appear customer oriented? Is there any form of guarantee to you as a consumer? Obviously no company can guarantee an exchange but to what extent do they remove the risk to you? Is your second year of membership free should you be unsuccessful in finding an exchange during your first year?

- What other value added benefits does the company offer with your membership? Can they provide insurance or discounts to other services in the travel industry?

Selecting a club off-line

If you're not using the internet, you can request printed literature from the prospective companies. Some of the above may apply to your decision making. In addition, ponder these points.

- Did a human answer the phone?

- Was the person taking your call able to handle your enquiry adequately?

- How quickly did you receive the requested information?

- Is the information professionally presented in a manner that is easy to understand?

- Is the information free of formatting and spelling errors?

- Does it appear that the company is knowledgeable about home swapping?

Getting the Edge on Finding the Right Exchange Partners

REGISTERING YOUR INTEREST

*S*o you've decided to opt for a formal club and you've identified the one that best suits your needs. The club application form will prompt you for all the information required of you.

This includes basic information about yourselves, the number of people in your travelling party, your approximate ages and specific ages of any accompanying children. It may ask you whether you smoke, whether you accept smokers in your home and whether you speak any foreign languages.

You need to state how other members can contact you. It is wise to provide all your details including your mailing address, telephone and fax numbers and your email address. If it is convenient to be contacted at work, you can provide a work number as well. Some listings include a mobile phone number but, in reality, few people would be prepared to make an international call to a mobile phone for the purpose of making an initial enquiry.

You will be asked to provide basic information about your home which includes the type of accommodation such as cottage, flat, semi-detached house; the number of storeys, bedrooms and bathrooms you offer and the number of guests your home can accommodate.

You may be given the opportunity to list any amenities you are offering your guests and to describe your immediate environs. The extent to which you are permitted to submit additional descriptive information depends on the club you select.

Finally, you will be invited to list some destination choices, an approximate timeframe, planned length of stay and the type of transaction you desire. If you are open to all offers, simply state that and you will undoubtedly receive plenty. Half the fun of home swapping is discovering exciting new destinations.

Your location and degree of flexibility are the most attractive aspects of your proposal, not the amenities of your home. Potential exchange guests aren't travelling the world to come and sit in your house. They won't select your property if it isn't otherwise attractive no matter how many gadgets and appliances you have. Make sure instead that you tout the attractions and unique aspects of your area and be as flexible with your timing and destination choices as possible.

A sample completed membership application (Table 6) is shown on the following page. If you join on-line, the format will be different but the questions will be similar.

Along with your application form, you'll be completing your registration details which include your payment information, selection of the service and options you require and any other marketing information the club requires of you such as how you heard of their service. You might be asked to agree to the club's Terms and Conditions. The registration details are not published in your listing.

What happens next depends on the service you have selected. If you've chosen custom matching, you now sit back and wait for your club to propose a property to you. If further information is required of you, the club will prompt you for it.

Table 6. Sample Completed Membership Application

MEMBERSHIP APPLICATION FORM

Title: Dr   **Last name:** Allen   **First name:** Julia

Title: Dr   **Last name:** Allen   **First name:** Martin

Exchange property address: 105 Todd Avenue

City: Ardross   **State/Country:** WA   **Postcode:** 6153

Mailing address (if different from above): _____

City: _____ **State/Country:** _____ **Postcode:** _____

Telephone: (08) 9364 6767   **Facsimile:** (08) 9364 4009

Email: allen@iinet.net.au   **How did you hear about us?** friend

Profession: Psychologists   **Former (if retired):** n/a

Reason for choosing home exchange: Save money on accom/privacy

ABOUT YOUR TRAVELLING PARTY

No. adults: 2 **Approx. ages:** 40s **No. children:** 2 **Ages:** 9, 11

Foreign languages: Some French

Car exchange? YES/~~NO~~ **Year, make, model:** 1998 Mitsubishi Lancer

Any smokers in your party? YES/~~NO~~ **Will you care for pets?** YES/~~NO~~

ABOUT YOUR HOME

Do you own it? YES/~~NO~~ **How many can it comfortably sleep?** 6

Property (house, flat): house **Setting (beach, village):** suburban

Nearest city: Perth **Distance:** 6 km **Views:** city glimpses

Metres^2: 200 **No. floors:** 2 **No. bedrooms:** 4 **No. bathrooms:** 2

Do you permit: Smoking? ~~YES~~/NO **Children?** YES/~~NO~~ **Pets?** ~~YES~~/NO

CIRCLE FEATURES/ACTIVITIES AVAILABLE TO YOUR GUESTS

garage • off-street parking • garden • patio • security features • jacuzzi • spa
pool • central heating • air-con • wheelchair access • TV • VCR • satellite
stereo/CD player • computer • fax • dishwasher • microwave • washing machine
dryer • gardener • cleaner • camping equipment • campervan • baby-sitting
bicycles • boat • restaurants • art gallery • library • shopping • museum • fishing
sailing • golf • tennis

Other: zoo, parks, walking tracks, theatre

Attractions of your area: see additional sheet

Please use additional paper to elaborate where necessary.

Destination(s): France, England, USA, Canada **Open to offers?** YES/~~NO~~

Length of exchange: 4-6 weeks

Exchange period: end Feb – Oct **Flexible?** YES/~~NO~~

If you have joined a club on-line, you should receive instructions allowing you to start searching for exchange properties immediately. If you've subscribed to a printed directory service, you await publication of the next edition. Some clubs provide back issues from which you can get started making selections.

EXPANDING ON YOUR PROPOSAL

Your proposal for an exchange has been registered and you now need to start preparing additional information to expand on this summary information. Some swappers provide only scant information while others put a great deal of effort into compiling information.

Remember, at this stage, you are still trying to attract other swappers to exchange with you. Potential swappers don't need to know your inside leg measurements or how to operate your microwave at this point. That comes later in the form of your 'fact file' which is left at your house for your incoming guests.

For now, the information you need to compile consists of the following items:

A sheet of photos showing your home and your travelling party

A letter of introduction describing your family

Character references

General information about your home

Expanded information about the merits of your environs

General climate information

Car and public transport details

Other relevant information

A sheet of photos showing your home and your travelling party

Take a roll of colour photos of the interior and exterior of your home and some of your travelling party. Make sure the photos provide an accurate representation of your home.

Select the best quality shots and arrange them on a standard sheet of paper. You can display four photos on one A4 sheet or eight photos on an A3 sheet (in North America 8.5″ x 11″ is the standard size). Take these to your local library or office supply store for colour copying. Many centres now have self-service machines for this purpose. To get even more photos on a page, set the copier machine to reduce the size of the photos.

At a couple of dollars a sheet, this is an inexpensive way of making several copies of your set of house photos. You will now have these readily available to send to prospective exchange partners.

A letter of introduction describing your family

Write a few paragraphs about your travelling party as an introduction to other club members. This need not be too personal but should have a friendly tone. Keep it concise.

By stating your own activities and interests, you tell others a little about yourselves as well as what's available in your environs. If you have swapped your home before, be sure to state this as it inspires confidence in potential exchange partners.

If you have a specific reason for selecting an area for an exchange, it may be worth stating this in your letter of introduction. This gives your potential exchange partners the opportunity to pick up on your needs and they may be able to assist you with them.

Tracy and William of Southport, Merseyside gave their reasons for choosing a specific location. *"Our reason for visiting Perth is to combine a holiday with the opportunity of seeing Western Australia before emigrating in a couple of years' time."* – which they did!

The following are samples of actual letters of introduction written by participants.

Sample 1. Bernard and Dora of Lancing, Sussex provide this letter of introduction to potential exchange partners.

My wife and I live in the large village of Lancing which is situated on the coast in the county of West Sussex. Our older children are independent and working in various parts of Europe but our younger daughter, Jessica, is still living at home and travelling with us.

I have been retired from working for the European Space Agency now for 18 months but for the time being my wife continues to give German lessons at the nearby school. We have spent a good part of our working lives in other countries, mainly Germany and the USA, which has given us a liking for warmer, dryer climates than one normally gets in England although it must be said that the last few years here have been exceptionally warm and dry.

We do a lot of reading, go occasionally to a classical musical concert, play squash and tennis, and do a lot of walking either on the promenades by the sea or in the open country side which begins immediately on the other side of the road in which we live.

Sample 2. Stephen of London describes his family and circumstances as follows:

I am looking for a home exchange in Sydney for May this year that can accommodate both myself and my partner and our daughter who will then be six months old. We would be happy to consider any property in the Sydney area which has at least one bedroom.

We are intending to be out of the UK from 30 April to 31 May inclusive. We are happy to consider a little flexibility on these dates.

The purpose of our stay is for a holiday and visiting relatives. As such we would be away from Sydney for a few days in the month. We are also intending a stopover in Bangkok on the way to Sydney and on the way home.

We are both lawyers in our mid-thirties and we have exchanged our home before. We can provide references from our previous exchange partners. We are non-smokers but we would allow smokers, children and possibly pets.

Character references

If you are new to home swapping, you will not yet have any references from previous exchange partners. Ask a neighbour, business associate or persons of good standing in your community to write a character reference for you. Provide actual written references rather than just the names of referees.

Ask your referee to state the nature and duration of your relationship and attest to your trustworthiness and suitability to the home swapping concept such as in the following samples.

Sample 1.

"I confirm that my husband and I have known Bernard and Dora as good friends and neighbours for over thirty years. They are entirely respectable and trustworthy and are persons quite suitable to be considered for any house-swapping arrangement."

Sample 2.

"I have known Professor and Mrs G. for several years and find them to be responsible citizens and good community members. I have no hesitation in confirming that they and their two children can be highly recommended for any home exchange program they may enter into."

Request that letterhead is used where available, make sure that the reference is dated and signed and that the referee's credentials are stated. Retain copies for further use.

Some people claim that references are 'not worth the paper they are written on'. This may or may not be true but consider this – in considering proposals for exchange, participants are more likely to select the party who appears well-organised and who has made some effort to prepare their information. It could be a reflection of how well they intend to prepare their home and provide for their exchange guests.

General information about your home

Describe your home in greater detail to give your potential exchange partners a better idea of what is on offer.

Vince of Cosham, Hampshire described his property and environs in a narrative:

The property is a three-bedroom semi-detached house located on the southern slopes of the South Downs, overlooking the City of Portsmouth with the Isle of Wight in the background. It is set back from the main road in a quiet and private location. There is a garage, off-road parking facilities and a 1989 Honda Accord automatic available for exchange. The medium sized garden has a patio area with barbeque facilities and a gardener attends weekly.

Many of the major tourist attractions in the South of England are accessible on a 'day trip' basis from Portsmouth, and the city itself, because of the centuries old naval connection, is a particular attraction to anyone interested in nautical matters.

Portsmouth is also a major ferry port with several shipping companies operating car ferries to France and Spain, making it a convenient jumping-off point for anyone wishing to visit the continent of Europe.

Local amenities include shops and a hospital within walking distance. Also a yacht marina, sports centre, golf clubs, bowling greens, ten pin bowling and other sports and recreational facilities are within easy reach.

Tracy and William gave a short description of their home and then listed their rooms:

Our home is situated 10 minutes walk from the town centre and is a large Victorian semi-detached, built in 1885. The house retains many of the original features including marble fireplaces, ceiling roses and architraving, but we have also attempted to modernise with features such as central heating and the addition of a sun room whilst preserving the character of the property.

<u>Ground floor</u>

Living room with feature marble fireplace

Sitting room with TV, video, etc.

Morning room with dining table, chairs, etc.

Kitchen with electric built-in oven, gas hob and microwave

Sun room containing wicker furniture

<u>First floor</u>

Master bedroom with fireplace. Can accommodate up to 5 people

Second bedroom with fireplace

Third bedroom

Bathroom with shower, toilet and wash basin

Separate WC

Centrally heated throughout

It is also useful to state the number and size of the beds in each of the rooms so that people considering your proposal can judge the suitability of the accommodation for their family.

An alternative is to provide a fact sheet, such as that provided by a real estate agent, listing the facilities by room as did Rob and Victoria of Guildford, Surrey.

DESCRIPTION

A Grade 11 listed period house, interesting and well maintained, believed to date from the 16th century with later additions. Stands in a lovely rural setting with southerly views over fields and beyond.

GROUND FLOOR

Oak front door leads to

ENTRANCE HALL coats hanging space, radiator

DRAWING ROOM 19' x 18'6" L-shaped, inglenook fireplace with concealed lighting and oak side seats, 3 radiators, fine old oak door to garden, exposed timbers, woodblock floor

DINING ROOM 19'8" x 12'; 2 radiators, hatch to kitchen, woodblock floor

REAR HALL deep shelved cupboard, Amtico tiled floor, door to rear porch and garden

SITTING ROOM 17'6" x 13'2" excellent full width unit incorporating cupboards, desk and display/book shelves, recessed ceiling lights, 2 radiators, woodblock floor, French doors to terrace and door to garage

UTILITY/CLOAKROOM 9' x 6'8" wc, sink, 2 double cupboards, Amtico tiled floor

FARMHOUSE KITCHEN/BREAKFAST ROOM 19'5" x 13' well fitted with custom made units of old pine incorporating double bowl stainless steel sink with waste disposal.

Adjoining work surfaces with cupboards and drawers under and wall cupboards above, fitted desk unit with glazed display cupboards above, shelved walk-in larder with light. Philips wall mounted electric oven and grill. Philips ceramic hob with extractor above. Oil fired Aga, part-tiled walls, Amtico tiled floor

FIRST FLOOR

LANDING linen cupboard, radiator

INNER LANDING deep cupboard, radiator

BEDROOM 1 16'9" x 15'7" excellent range of shelved and hanging cupboards with further cupboards above, eaves cupboards, two radiators, rural views

DRESSING ROOM/BEDROOM 6 12'1" X 9'2" full width range of shelved and hanging cupboards (one housing lagged hot water cylinder and immersion heater), further cupboards above and central wash basin with cupboards under and lights/shaver point

BATHROOM 1 bath with shower, wash basin, wc, bidet, heated towel rail, radiator, part tiled walls

Note: The above 3 rooms are approached from the inner landing and form an excellent self-contained suite

BEDROOM 2 13'8" x 10'6" shelved and hanging wardrobe cupboard, wash basin in vanity unit with cupboards under, radiator

BEDROOM 3 12'4" x 9'9" shelved and hanging wardrobe cupboard, wash basin in vanity unit with cupboards under, window seat, bookshelves, radiator

BEDROOM 4 14' x 13'2" two deep wardrobe cupboards, wash basin, radiator, features south facing oriel bay window

BEDROOM 5 10'3" x 6'6" display shelves, radiator, wash basin

BATHROOM 2 bath with newly fitted limed oak bath panel, wash basin in marble surround with limed oak cupboards under, wc, bidet, heated towel rail, airing cupboard with lagged hot water cylinder and immersion heater, recessed lighting, strip light/shaver point, access to roof space via folding ladder and extensive storage

OUTSIDE

OLD TIMBER FRAMED PERIOD BARN Reconstructed and restored in 1983 of old elm frame with weatherboarding under a clay peg-tiled pitched roof, wide double elm doors, side door to garden, electric light and power

INTEGRAL DOUBLE GARAGE 18'6" x 15'8" two double timber doors, light, power, extensive shelving

BRICK AND TILE WORKSHOP 8' x 8'

GARDEN STORE

GARDEN At the front is a five barred gate and old stone wall with sweeping gravelled drive besides lawns, wide stone path to the front door and a beautiful herbaceous border with pergola and climbing roses. At the rear is a paved terrace and lawns with lovely old oak, weeping willow, eucalyptus, maple, chestnut, several fruit trees and well stocked borders. An opening through a cupressus hedge leads to the vegetable garden with soft fruit cage. Beyond is a small orchard. Garden is extremely well maintained and adjoins fields on two sides providing a lovely rural atmosphere. Approx 1 acre in all.

SITUATION

Littleton is a lovely old hamlet, well off the beaten track and originally the community connected to the historic Elizabethan Losely House and Park. The house stands in a country lane which runs through fields and is lined with many period houses in an area of outstanding natural beauty.

In the centre of the village is the picturesque church of St. Francis, part of which was originally built by the village school. From the lane, there is direct access onto the North Downs and Pilgrims Way providing miles of lovely walking and riding countryside.

Littleton lies under two miles south of Guildford town centre where there are excellent shopping, educational and recreational facilities and the main line station provides a fast service to Waterloo in 30 minutes. The A3 connecting with the M25 road network is within 2 miles and Heathrow and Gatwick Airports are reached within 30 minutes. Littleton is unique in the area for its peaceful rural atmosphere yet within minutes of Guildford.

Guildford Town Centre – 2 miles

Waterloo - 30 mins

Godalming – 2.5 miles

A3 – 2 miles

M25 – 7 miles

London – 30 miles

Expanded information about the merits of your environs

Here you can list the primary activities and amenities of your area. Try to keep this relevant to your target exchange population.

For example, if you know you will be swapping with a family with school age children for several months, you might include details of the type of schools and the respective distances from your home. If, on the other hand, you will definitely not be accepting children in your home, there would be little point in exalting the merits of child-related amenities.

If retirees are your intended exchange target group, state the kinds of activities and amenities likely to be enjoyed and utilised by seniors. These might include bowls clubs, golf courses, bridge clubs, churches or a doctor's surgery.

List only those festivals and events that will be occurring during your intended departure.

General climate information

Provide some basic information about the characteristic weather in your area, for example, temperature, rainfall and snowfall. Make sure you accurately portray the information for the period of your intended departure. Potential swappers won't be interested in the unusual warmth of your recent summer if you're expecting them to come in the height of your winter.

Car and public transport details

If you are offering a car, state the make, model and year. Give an indication of its current odometer reading and its general condition. State whether it has a manual or an automatic transmission.

Include details about the type and availability of public transport. Provide information about the closest airports and the distances from your home. Outline suggested modes of transport from the airport to your home and the approximate costs.

Other relevant information

Explain any special circumstances such as a permanent tenant in a self-contained granny flat. You may have special needs such as adapted equipment in the bathroom or perhaps your home is suitable for the needs of a disabled traveller. State those items here.

What not to say

It is vital not to embellish the details of your offer and to give as honest a description as possible.

Graham of Brighton, England enjoyed his trip to Sydney, escaping the British winter. *"I was very satisfied but more information would have been helpful to avoid unreal expectations. The flat was noisy, close to a new flight path which the owners had neglected to mention. I still would have exchanged!"*

Similar comments were made by Peter and Jean of Sussex. *"The house was more or less as described except for the level of noise from an extremely busy dual carriageway. It was horrendous. No double glazing or proper curtains meant that we were woken every morning at 5.30 by daylight and traffic noise. Because of these two factors, sleeping arrangements were poor."*

John and Brenda from Kidderminster were bitterly disappointed in their first exchange. *"The described views were 4.5 kilometres away and only the top of the skyscrapers could be seen from the unit balcony. The description stated that the home was heated by radiators but there were none. It stated there was a garden, patio and barbeque facilities but there was no garden, no patio and no barbeque. So it didn't matter that there was also no gardener as stated.*

The noise of the traffic just 60 metres away made sleep impossible without the windows closed. Had we known that this was not our hosts' home but just a holiday unit with bare necessities, we would never have agreed to the exchange."

Equally important is not omitting important items. One couple listed all the usual kitchen appliances including fridge, microwave and even a freezer. Their guests were naturally surprised to discover that they'd failed to mention that there was actually no kitchen.

"My wife repeatedly opened doors to a broom closet, a toilet and various cupboards before the reality finally set in that there was no

kitchen. The major appliances they had listed in their description were all there – and could be found in the strangest places."

Try to avoid sole use of capital letters in your correspondence, especially when using email. It gives the respondent the notion that you are 'shouting' at them.

If you have stated 'no smoking' or 'no children' in your listing, leave it at that. There is no need to slight the intelligence of other members by making too much of what has already been said.

One listing contained three full paragraphs ranting about the owners' already stated stipulation that no smokers stay in their home. It was quite objectionable, even to non-smokers.

Adopt the view that members respect the wishes of others and that they will read the details of your listing before contacting you. Later, you will have the opportunity to confirm your preferences with your selected exchange partners.

Make sure that your description gives an accurate account of what is actually available to your guests. It is important not to tout your home as having three bedrooms if, in fact, only two will be available to your guests. If a bedroom is used as a study or a sewing room, make sure it isn't listed as a bedroom and indicate whether the room will be available to your guests. It is quite acceptable to have an off-limits room but your potential guests need to be informed in advance.

Similarly, if you have stated that no children are accepted, there is little point in plugging the local playground facilities.

If your garage will house your car during the exchange because you are not planning to make it available to your guests, you should leave out that you have a garage altogether. Only state what is going to be available to your guests.

Finally, be careful when making claims about the level of accessibility of your home to the disabled. Wheelchairs users require a specified minimum door width, adequate floor space to manoeuvre within the rooms and, depending on the individual circumstances, may require ramps and other structural adaptations. Your two storey house with all the bedrooms and bathrooms on the upper level is *not* considered wheelchair accessible. Unless you are absolutely certain that your home is wheelchair accessible, it's best to leave this out.

IDENTIFYING POTENTIAL EXCHANGE PARTNERS

Now you can begin to identify potential exchange partners. Allow adequate time to arrange your exchange because once you've narrowed down the options and found the party with whom you'll exchange, you'll still need plenty of time to correspond with them before the exchange actually takes place.

If you're working from a directory, start marking the offers which attract you the most. You may wish to establish some form of ranking system based on factors which best meet your original criteria.

Don't be put off if the stated destinations and timeframe do not match your own at this point. Many people who start with very definite ideas ultimately become more flexible as their travel dates approach – or when they discover from their contact with others that their original criteria were too rigid. Still others state specific destinations and dates merely because the application form prompts them to do so.

If you're searching on the internet, you'll have to test the waters of your chosen club's web site. There should be a full explanation of how its search engine works. If not, ask the club.

Start by entering a few keywords which most apply to the exchange you seek. If you get too many hits, try narrowing it down by adding more keywords. If you don't get enough hits, try widening your search by decreasing the number of keywords.

On most sites, you can 'click for more information' which will expand on the raw information provided in the summary. Print out a list of selected properties to review off-line. You can now discard the unsuitable ones and make direct contact with those of interest to you.

Now that you have read the listings of other members, this may be a good time to review your own listing. You may have discovered that your own request appears inflexible or perhaps you're prompted to expand on it somewhat. Keep it friendly and inviting.

You will benefit from taking an active approach and contacting other members rather than the more passive approach of waiting for others to contact you. It is, to some extent, a numbers game so contact as many people as possible.

You will find that some will not reply at all, others will have made plans already and, hopefully, some will reply favourably showing interest in your offer. Of the latter, further correspondence may reveal some obstacles which cannot be overcome such as with timing and so they too will be eliminated in favour of the most ideal.

Communicating with Your Exchange Partners

*S*uccessful exchanges begin with open communication. Once you've found one or more potential parties, it is time to begin corresponding. It is important to be completely honest about your intentions, especially where you are undecided between several offers.

It is equally important to reply to all expressions of interest, even if only in the form of a postcard or email with a brief line politely declining. This is a courtesy appreciated by everyone. It can be quite disheartening to be completely ignored.

As negotiations progress towards an exchange between two parties, you might like to provide supporting documents such as your character references from neighbours or previous exchange guests, or copies of title/mortgage statements for proof of ownership.

In cases where rental properties are being exchanged, obtain written permission from the landlord or owner of each property authorising the exchange and stating that the rent is paid by standing order.

Some participants send video tapes of themselves, their homes and cars. Extend an invitation to your potential exchange partners to appoint a local representative to come and meet you and inspect your home prior to finalising any arrangements. You may have friends or relatives in your exchange destination that could act as your representative. This will give you some feedback about your potential hosts as well as help to put everyone at ease.

Express your concerns to your exchange partners and be forthright about any off-limits areas or items.

Soon you will feel like old friends. It doesn't matter what kind of arrangements you make, as long as you have discussed them and agreed to them, preferably *in writing* prior to the exchange.

HOW TO GET IN TOUCH

How you correspond with potential swappers will be determined by the means of communication available to both parties.

Electronic mail (email) is the medium of choice. Because transmission is immediate, you won't have to wait days or weeks for a postal mail reply and there is no chance of disturbing the recipient due to differing time zones.

Furthermore, to reply costs nothing and requires almost no effort on the part of the recipient. Therefore, even if they are unable to accept your offer, you are far more likely to get a reply politely declining your offer.

The next most convenient and expedient means is by fax. If the party you are contacting lists neither a fax number nor an email address, you need to resort to phone calls and traditional mail services.

It is recommended that one or two letters are exchanged before any international telephone calls are made. An unexpected phone call can sometimes take people off-guard.

Once a few letters have been exchanged, whether by email or snail mail, it is a good idea to make a couple of telephone calls to discuss those last minute items. The exchange holiday is probably going to save you thousands of dollars – a couple of long distance phone calls will go a long way to giving you peace of mind by providing personal contact.

COMMUNICATION TIPS

The following are a few general communication tips for contacting other exchangers.

Regardless of whether you are using email or traditional mail, it is important to properly identify yourself and make your initial proposal clear.

Initial proposals should address the person to whom you are writing by name, include your own full name and your membership number if you have one, state where you saw the listing and provide a brief outline of your proposal.

Email tends to bring out the informal nature in us, but try to resist sending 'one liners' such as:

"Hi. Would you like to swap with us? You can find our listing on Page 54."

You are unlikely to get a reply. You need to elicit sufficient interest to encourage the recipient to read about your offer and to make it easy for them to find details of your proposal.

Another temptation to resist is sending huge photo files with a preliminary email enquiry. Send only a few views initially, enough to spark some interest. If the person is not even interested in the basics of your proposal, they won't appreciate excessive attachment files clogging up their hard drives and taking lengthy periods to download.

A good approach is to offer to attach photos if they are interested or to send just one small photo file with your initial enquiry. For transmitting via the internet, photo files should be kept small in file size (approximately 1KB); in physical size (approximately 2.3" x 1.5") and in resolution (no greater than 100). JPEG (.jpg) is the file format of choice. These parameters will ensure fast transmission that won't inconvenience the recipient.

Alternatively, if you have your own web site or a home page, you can of course refer to it here and provide a link. If interested, the recipient simply clicks on the link and is automatically taken to your web page.

SAMPLE LETTERS AND FORMS

In this section, you will find sample letters which you may like to adapt to your particular situation. These cover the various stages of negotiating an exchange.

1. Expression of interest

2. Letter of regret

3. Confirmation of interest

4. Confirmation of exchange agreement

5. Letter of appreciation

6. Backing out of an agreement

1. Expression of interest

5 Feb

9 Stanley Close
High Wycombe
Bucks
HP13 5TN

Tel: 01844.275999
Email: gmmullen@hotmail.com

Dear George and Marie,

We have seen your listing on the Latitudes Home Exchange web site. The purpose of writing is to express our interest in the possibility of exchanging homes with you and to determine whether our proposal might be of interest to you. If you do not have internet access, you can find our listing on page 25 of the November directory.

A little about us – we are a married couple with two teenage children (Sarah aged 15 and Julian aged 13). We are non-smokers and our children are house-trained and respectful of the property of others. Simon is a Veterinary Surgeon and I am a part-time Speech Pathologist.

We have a cosy home in a small village just outside the market town of High Wycombe. There are excellent bus and rail links to central London (about 40 minutes by rail) as well as to Windsor, Oxford, Reading and both Heathrow and Gatwick airports. The nearby M40 motorway connects to London, Oxford and the Cotswolds.

Our preferred timeframe would be for the month of August but we're open between mid-July and early September since that's when we have our school summer holidays. We'd like to exchange for about 4 weeks but we're flexible in this regard.

We enclose some colour photocopies of the family and some of our house. We'd really appreciate a brief reply even if you don't think you'd be interested. If you'd also return our photos, this would be a real bonus.

(We've included our fax and email details in case you have access to a fax machine or email through work). Looking forward to hearing from you.

Best wishes,
Simon and Lisa Mullen
Member reference number: LT-012-GBE-2999

2. Letter of regret

11 Feb

37 Seaview Road
Paremata, Wellington 6006
New Zealand   *Tel: 04.233.4931*

Dear Simon and Lisa,

Thanks so much for your letter. Your area sounds really interesting but we have just committed ourselves to an exchange in Scotland for this year. I'm enclosing your colour copies as requested. Good luck with your exchange hunting.

Regards,
George Dixon

3. Confirmation of interest

2 Feb

4 Hillcrest Avenue
South Perth
Western Australia 6151   *Tel: (08) 9367.8888*

Dear Mandy and Rob,

Thanks for your letter. Yes, we are very interested in your proposal, it sounds ideal for us. We didn't think we'd be lucky enough to get our choice of location and timing on our first exchange attempt!

I am enclosing some additional information that we have prepared to expand on our listing. This gives an outline of our family, our home and the immediate area. Of course, we'll add to this as time goes on and answer any questions you have as they arise.

It is interesting that your daughter is living and working quite near to us. She would be most welcome to come over and meet us and inspect our house on your behalf. Please feel free to pass on our telephone number so that we can arrange a mutually convenient time. Looking forward to further discussion.

Best wishes,
Julia Cobb

4. Confirmation of exchange agreement

4 Feb

7 Brennan Drive
Port Dover
Ontario N0A 1N0   *Tel: 519.111.2222*

Dear John and Maggie,

We were delighted to learn that you would like to go ahead with an exchange with us. We can now confirm that we are also definitely committed to proceeding with you. To this end, we have now written to the other parties with whom we had been corresponding, to advise them that we have made this decision.

We've also made some preliminary enquiries with the airlines which proved satisfactory. John has also put in for the time off work and that looks like being no problem either.

We are both getting really excited about this exchange and we've started making a list of the things we need to discuss with you. More about this as soon as we can confirm the above.

Regards,
Julia Wagner

5. Letter of appreciation

20 Oct

44 Pearson Way
Launceston
Tasmania

Dear Paul and Marilynne,

A brief note to say a sincere 'thank you'. Thank you for allowing us the use of your home and vehicle, which has provided us with lifetime memories of our wonderful three weeks on Vancouver Island.

Thank you also for the way you left our own property and vehicle. We were careful and respectful of yours, and obviously you were the same here. Yet another home exchange appears to have been successfully concluded.

We hope you enjoyed your time in Tassie, the Olympics and New Zealand. We certainly enjoyed ourselves in your area. Whilst we have pretty much "done" Vancouver Island, I understand there are parts of Tasmania that you didn't get to see. That being the case, should you decide to return sometime in the future to see the rest, Joy and I would be pleased to offer you, as a minimum, complimentary B&B in our home. Just let us know. It would be nice to actually meet you both face to face!

Regards,
Bob and Joy

6. Backing out of an agreement

6 Nov

11243 Julian Road
Mesa, Arizona 85213

Dear Mark and Sue,

It was with deep regret that we had to inform you that we will not be able to proceed with our agreed upon plans. We were so sorry to have to 'drop this on you' out of the blue on the telephone but we felt we should let you know immediately we found out. We are so disappointed because we were looking forward to the trip but also we were feeling that we were just getting to know you and we feel terrible to have to let you down.

As mentioned to you on the phone, it was only through a routine physical by our GP that revealed Dave has this problem and the doctor definitely advises against travel. Now that the initial shock of it is over, we have had a bit more time to contemplate ways that we can try and fulfil our obligation to you. We really hate letting you down at this stage. Although it seems we cannot travel ourselves because of the need to stay close to home for the treatment and further tests, we have some possible solutions for your consideration.

As you know, we have the holiday home which is only a two hour drive from here. You are more than welcome to make use of it during the time we'd planned to swap if that would be acceptable to you. It's only a second home but our son and his wife (who live quite close) will endeavour to make sure it is kitted out just like a main home. If this doesn't sound suitable but you are able to change your flight dates, we could keep the offer of this house open for another time. After Dave's treatment is finished, we will probably go south for a recuperation period. During that time, you could use this house. Naturally, these dates would have to be confirmed at a later date but the offer is there if it would help you out.

Alternatively, you might have time to simply find an alternative exchange party. Regardless of what you decide, you will be very welcome to avail yourselves of our homes when it can be fitted in and we will not require any reciprocal arrangements. We would just feel a lot better if something could be worked out for you.

Once again, we are so sorry that this has happened and hope to have your thoughts soon.

Best wishes,
Jan Peterson

Issues to Address with Your Exchange Partners

*Y*ou have now agreed upon the exchange. It is time to establish your own unique guidelines and expand upon the preliminary information already provided. The following topics need to be addressed and documented.

Meeting your guests

Maps

Keys

Telephone charges

Utility bill obligations

Use of household supplies

Mail handling

Linens and towels

Repairs and maintenance

Absences and additional guests

Home and contents insurance

Car exchange and insurance

Contingency plans

Pets

Gardening and plant care

Finalising dates and confirming airline bookings

MEETING YOUR GUESTS

Is anyone available to meet your guests at the airport or station? The exchange dates may not coincide exactly, which may give you the opportunity to meet your exchange partners at the beginning or end of the stay. Perhaps you prefer to make this arrangement anyway, so that you can get acquainted and explain the general running of the home.

Barbara and Norman of Katoomba, New South Wales met their London exchange partners before and after their swap. Barbara says: "*Meeting the people, or at least talking by 'phone, makes you feel that you are just having friends over.*"

Many participants have commented that, having met their exchange partners, any fears they had were instantly dispelled, and they felt confident that they were leaving their home in good hands. Jan and Peter of Moora, Western Australia had this to say: "*Our exchange to England was so successful. Their house was ideal for our purpose and we were lucky enough to spend an evening with the owners before they flew out.*"

Their exchange partners agreed that there was value in meeting each other. "*Jan and Peter hired a car and drove to our house to meet us prior to our departure with the intention of staying in a hotel that first night. We invited them to spend the night with us and then felt confident about leaving our house in their hands. The dates matched so well that we were able to collect them from the airport at the end of the exchange and compare our experiences the day before we left Australia.*"

Chris and Ken of Tasmania co-ordinated their trip dates so perfectly that their exchange guests left on the same plane that brought them home. "*Our car was washed and polished and waiting outside the airport entrance. We had a brief hello and goodbye with Terry and Joan.*"

Cynthia and Brian of Wanaka, New Zealand have also met most of their exchange partners. *"On one exchange, we arrived on the plane that was taking our exchange partners to our country so we literally had a few moments to say hello and then they were off. We've had other experiences where we've spent one night before the other couple left. It can be nerve racking at first but once you've actually done it, you can realise the value in it."*

If it doesn't work out that you can meet personally, or if you are the party arriving at the destination first, try to arrange for a friend or family member to greet your guests. After a long plane trip, it is very comforting to know that someone will be at the destination to meet you.

Geoff and Judith of Risdon Vale, Tasmania agree: *"The home was so comfortable and welcoming. Their son-in-law picked us up and returned us to the airport. I would give them ten out of ten for their hospitality and kindness to us."*

Make your neighbours aware that there will be people living in your home. Encourage and arrange for them to meet. Try to avoid arranging hospitality for your guests on their first night where possible. They may be tired and will probably prefer to be left to their own devices to get settled in, especially after a long journey.

Ron of Whitby, Yorkshire had originally requested a mutual mid-term inspection to be organised by family members. Having met his exchange partners before departure, he decided there was no need at all. Indeed, what begins as a business transaction with strangers inevitably evolves into a trusting friendship.

MAPS

If your guests must make their own way to your home, ensure that you send adequate maps and instructions detailing how to get from the airport or station to your home.

KEYS

Decide how to exchange keys. This can be done in person, via the mail or through a neighbour or relative. Discuss where or with whom the keys should be left at the end of the stay. State where spare keys can be obtained.

If you are appointing someone to hand over the keys, make sure they have two sets; one to give your exchange guests and another set that they can retain. It is quite common for exchangers to lock themselves out of an unfamiliar home.

TELEPHONE CHARGES

Discuss payment of telephone bills. If the exchange is for a lengthy period, you might wish to change the account names. Remember that you would be paying a telephone line rental rate even if your home were left empty.

Usually, the host pays the base line rental and the guests pay any local or long distance charges. These can be settled up at the end of the exchange period by exchanging photocopies of the bills with each other. With call details now widely itemised, identifying who made the call is a simple matter.

It is also possible to settle your bill with the telephone company prior to your departure and have your guests do the same when they leave your house.

Remember that each country has its own cost structure for local calls. If you live in the USA, you'll be accustomed to making unlimited local calls of any length for free. Your exchange partners may not be so fortunate. In England, for instance, local calls are time charged so be mindful of this when using the phone especially if your exchange partners are providing internet access for you.

In Australia, there is a standard fee for each local call irrespective of its length. This rate varies from company to company. Local calls are not itemised on the bill but it is now possible to subscribe to a free service with some phone companies which allows you to access your itemised local calls on their web site.

Swappers George and Penny of Dover, England bought a phone card and walked down to the public phone to make any calls. They advised that *British Telecom* cards could be purchased in the UK.

UK exchangers Bob and Joyce buy a phone card when they get to Australia. This card allows them to make calls back to the UK at a rate as cheap, or cheaper, than most phone companies offer their local customers. The phone card does not have to be inserted into a public call box but can be used from any home phone.

Joyce says that cards of various denominations are available. She purchases a $20 card. By dialling a series of code numbers, she can access the network and, at the conclusion of the call, an automatic message advises how much credit remains.

Australians Cecil and Joan of Caloundra, Queensland bought a *Telstra* phone card before they left and all their calls were debited back to their home account which Joan says was most convenient. The Canadians with whom they swapped made similar arrangements with their phone company.

Adrian and Marian of Easter Compton, Avon said: "*We left the issue of phone bills fairly open though we agreed to pay for our own long distance calls. Our exchange guests left cash to cover the cost of international calls made.*"

Some mobile phones can be used overseas. Check the call charges before making any calls back home though as these can be quite prohibitive. Due to the 'creative fee structuring' devised by some mobile phone companies, you may find yourself paying international rates just to make a local call while overseas.

UTILITY BILL OBLIGATIONS

Decide who will be responsible for utility bills and how they will be paid. Consider establishing an agreed usage rate, based on your own normal consumption. In the case of lengthy exchanges, you may wish to change the account names.

Some participants simply pay the bill at their own home especially where the exchange is for a shorter term. Remember that there would be some standing costs incurred even if your home was left vacant. Perhaps you can arrange to each put up a bond to cover utilities.

Both parties should settle their bills at their own home prior to leaving. Then, settle up the differences in expenses at the end of the exchange period. How this is achieved depends on the individuals involved.

Many survey participants reported having no such formal agreements. Pat and Paul of Newtown, Tasmania admitted: "*We made no special arrangements about utility bills and we each paid for the power in our own home. As it turned out, we got the best of the deal but they refused our offer to pay for the imbalance.*" They'd travelled to Christchurch, Dorset for a month-long exchange.

Some swappers simply exchange bills at the end of the stay. Others agree that the difference between the two bills will be paid by the party incurring the charges. Still others accept that they will pay the bills at their own home providing the amount doesn't exceed ten per cent of their normal usage for the time of year.

Bob and Joy of Tasmania who've swapped several times noted: *"We never worry about power costs. The first people we swapped with insisted on meter readings before and after the exchange for both gas and electricity. The difference in consumption costs were negligible – a few dollars at most. We don't think it's worth the hassle of getting meter readings."*

Joan, a Director of Nursing from Perth, who swapped with members in San Francisco reported, *"My electricity bill was three times the usual amount but we put many more miles on their car than they did on mine so it evened out."*

USE OF HOUSEHOLD SUPPLIES

State how you wish to handle the use and replacement of your household supplies. Adrian and Marian of Easter Compton, Avon agreed with their exchange partners to use up general household items before replacing them.

MAIL HANDLING

Decide how you would like your incoming mail to be handled. If you ask your Post Office to hold or forward *all* mail until your return, remember that your guests will not receive their mail either!

LINENS AND TOWELS

Discuss arrangements for linens and towels. It is customary to supply these items for your guests. No-one wants to fill a suitcase with sheets and towels when travelling.

REPAIRS AND MAINTENANCE

Discuss how repairs and maintenance should be handled. It is important to keep in mind that we all live differently. You might think it odd that your exchange guests don't have a grab bar to haul themselves out of the bath tub but they won't necessarily appreciate your handyman efforts to provide them with one! You need to have a fairly good feel for each other before making structural alterations.

Chris, a widow from Kings Langley, Hertfordshire travelling with a teenage daughter was delighted to find odd jobs had been carried out at her house by her Adelaide, South Australia counterparts. *"It was the perfect exchange. We got on so well with Max and Shirley and felt like old friends right from the start. Everything was just as we left it, all spotlessly clean and no damage. Max had even fitted us a security light and done some small household jobs. We were very happy."*

On the other hand, if an item gets damaged as a result of your stay, it is essential that you move to make proper restoration. If you aren't really too handy, it is better to engage the services of a professional. You can usually find local trades people listed by specific trade in community newspapers, shop front windows, libraries or, less locally, look in the phone book.

ABSENCES AND ADDITIONAL GUESTS

Let your host know if you plan to be absent from their home for more than a few nights. Secure their permission if you intend to entertain overnight guests at their home. Be honest about the number and ages of people in your travelling party. If you have agreed on no children in your exchange, obtain the owner's permission if you intend entertaining your own under age family members (such as grandchildren) in the exchange home.

HOME AND CONTENTS INSURANCE

Insurance companies recognise the value of having someone living in your home and many actually suspend the contents coverage on homes left vacant for prolonged periods. The definition of 'prolonged periods' will vary from insurer to insurer.

Your home is usually insured for your exchange guests as if you were living in it yourself. It would be unusual for an insurance company not to embrace the concept of home exchange.

Check with your insurance agent to ensure that you have the appropriate insurance coverage and that your home owner's policy will be valid while your exchange partners are in residence. Make sure your insurance agent realises that your exchange partners are non-paying guests.

Swappers have recommended that these issues be addressed early in the planning as, especially in Britain, some insurance agents are very slow to finalise documentation. Leave your insurance agent's particulars for your guests in case of emergency. Make sure that anything stated by the insurance company is confirmed in writing.

Insurance claims concerning theft are rarely met unless there is evidence of forced entry. Reports of theft or intentional damage are extremely rare, but even the most careful guests have minor breakages, which are usually replaced by the offender.

Major appliance failure, such as a washing machine or fridge, is the responsibility of the host. Be aware that fusion of motors on major appliances could be covered by home owner's insurance.

Provide your exchange guests with instructions on how to properly secure your home.

CAR EXCHANGE AND INSURANCE

Exchanging cars is often an issue of greater concern than making a home available to strangers. It is important to extend understanding when negotiating the details of car exchange. Be respectful of the owners' concerns and restrictions.

If car exchange is agreed upon, ensure that you have the appropriate insurance. It is usually sufficient to notify your insurer that you would like additional names listed on your policy to drive your vehicle. Some insurers require a photocopy of the overseas driving licence. They usually require the name, date of birth and details of any driving convictions for each additional overseas driver.

More meticulous companies may require the guest drivers to complete a 'Supplementary Declaration In Respect Of Additional Drivers'. They will need the names and dates of birth of the additional drivers who will be asked to make a signed declaration concerning any previous disqualifications; convictions in the past five years; related physical impairments and disabilities such as vision or hearing loss, epilepsy; whether motor insurance has ever been declined and details of any accidents, claims and losses in the past three years.

Participants in England have noted that some insurance agents took a long time to confirm the approval of additional drivers. Returning from their exchange to Perth, Australia, George and Penny of Dover, England recommended that members *"…investigate matters regarding car insurance early in the planning stages of the exchange. Our UK insurance carrier was slow to respond and this issue was not finalised until we were almost ready to leave."*

It is also reported that some UK insurance companies refuse to cover American drivers.

Don of Swindon, Wiltshire had an uneasy feeling when his exchange partners were unable to provide documented evidence of car insurance. *"Len never really provided any real 'hard' evidence that my wife and I were insured to drive his car in New Zealand. There was no information about RAC or other breakdown services. He didn't respond to this question before we left and his family were unable to help with it on our arrival. Fortunately, there were no problems but it left a sense of unease."*

Bud and Lorene are Americans living in Australia. Their recommendations for anyone considering a car exchange include the following advice about insurance: *"Make sure you know exactly what insurance your exchanger has particularly with respect to the car. Don't assume, especially if it's their first exchange, that they will look after your needs. You must be forthright with questions in this regard."*

The owner should be responsible for routine maintenance. Any damage incurred is the responsibility of the driver, who would be expected to pay any deductibles. Decide on a maximum payable for damage before a claim will be made because it is not worth forfeiting a no-claim bonus for a relatively small sum. Decide who will be responsible for repairs.

Harold and Barbara of Minyama Waters, Queensland were advised that their car had sustained a cracked windshield but their English guests had already covered the costs of the repairs by the time they found out. Similarly, John of Golden Beach, Queensland noted, *"A minor accident to our car was very well repaired. We hadn't even realised it had happened until it was mentioned in a letter."*

It is important to outline any geographical or mileage restrictions that you wish to impose. If you live in Australia, for example, you might state that you do not wish your car driven across the Nullarbor Plain. It may be necessary to further explain the extreme conditions encountered in certain parts of Australia during the summer months. Visitors from colder climes may be oblivious to the hazards of driving a car in temperatures in excess of 40°C.

Equally, if your vehicle is based in England, you may have to explain to your exchange guests that your insurance will not cover them for trips to the Continent. Or, if your home borders with Mexico, you'll need to explain that it is illegal to drive in Mexico without first securing Mexican insurance.

John and Jenny of Caloundra, Queensland filed the following report about the use of their car: *"The car to our way of thinking was used excessively and a total of 8200 kilometres was clocked up. This averaged out over 80 kilometres per day.*

Although not externally damaged, we found that the shock absorbers were faulty, the car was full of rattles and had obviously been left in the scorching sun for lengthy periods. A seat belt bracket was broken and the hatch cover piece damaged. We have since traded this car and were told that because of the excess mileage, we lost $500 on the trade."

Cynthia and husband Brian, a retired General Motors franchisee, of Wanaka disagree: *"We feel that extra mileage on a car at the time of resale makes absolutely no difference to the price we can achieve so we just don't worry about it. In our experience, most of the exchangers have been more concerned about the use of their car than their homes.*

We find that the insurance company raises the excess (deductible) for overseas drivers over 55 years. We tell our exchangers this in advance and get them to agree that if there's a problem they will pay the excess."

Peter and Leonie of Ohope, New Zealand chose to rent a car and use local trains rather than exchange cars because they knew they would be clocking up excessive mileage during their exchange to England.

CONTINGENCY PLANS

It is important to discuss contingency plans with your exchange partners in the event of ill health. If one party changes the terms of the agreement, they should assume full responsibility for making alternative arrangements to house their guests. They also need to take responsibility for the care of the guests' own property during their absence.

If you are the party forced to cancel the arrangements because of illness or the death of your travelling partner, the last thing you want to deal with is finding alternative accommodation for your exchange partners. Encourage them to deal with this issue also. Having an alternative strategy planned well in advance makes obvious sense.

If yours is an unsynchronised exchange, what provisions has the first family made in the event that the home intended for your use gets sold in the meantime? Ask for a commitment in writing confirming contingency plans. These might include the use of their primary residence or perhaps financial reimbursement for the time they spent at your home.

Decide what each of you will do to accommodate the other should the need arise to cancel. This might entail offering to share accommodation if the home is large enough and provides adequate privacy. There might be provision for the use of a second home.

Depending on the circumstances, you might consider moving out to accommodate your guests. If someone in your travelling party were too ill to travel, it would be unlikely you'd be in a position to vacate the premises. Would there be a family member in the area who could help out by providing accommodation under these circumstances?

Perhaps you can both agree to a form of financial compensation if either is forced to cancel. This money would be spent on commercial lodging for the let-down party.

It is wise to take out some form of travel cancellation insurance just as you would when planning any overseas trip. Last minute problems will ruin your holiday and cost you dearly if you have nowhere to stay.

Through an affiliation with one of the world's leading insurance companies, at *Latitudes Home Exchange,* we were able to offer our members a comprehensive travel insurance policy at competitive rates.

This policy was specifically written to address the unique needs of home exchangers and even included a specific clause providing cover in the unlikely event that the exchange partners were forced to cancel. It might be possible for individuals to independently negotiate such a clause with their insurance company.

Although difficult to legally enforce, each party needs to fully understand their obligations and responsibilities with respect to making a firm exchange agreement.

PETS

If your exchange guests have agreed to care for your pet, outline the care needs and provide the vet's details for emergencies. Establish a designated person who can take over the pet care should your guests wish to travel away from your home for a few nights.

If you have been asked to care for a pet but really don't want the responsibility, it is better to state your feelings on the matter than proceed with the plans feeling resentful or concerned.

On the other hand, temporary access to a pet could really enhance the holiday through the eyes of a child.

GARDENING AND PLANT CARE

Outline any gardening expectations prior to the exchange. Most people don't mind watering a few houseplants but don't want to spend their holidays mowing lawns and weeding gardens. If you have a lawn mowing service, it is wise to keep this going at your own expense in your absence.

THEY'VE ASKED, WOULD WE MIND DOING A BIT OF PRUNING!

Joan from Perth who went to California remarked: '*If there was a downside it was that gardening was a hassle on a steep slope with poison ivy. But any disadvantages were far outweighed by the overall positive experience.*"

If you have an automatic sprinkler system, leave the user's manual and make sure there is a contact person named for repairs. Be aware of differing climes and that your incoming guests may not understand the effects of local weather conditions on your garden.

FINALISING DATES AND CONFIRMING AIRLINE BOOKINGS

During all your negotiations, you will have had at least a rough idea of the proposed timing of the exchange. Perhaps one party had firm dates from the outset. In this case, the other will have been making enquiries of the airlines to reserve coinciding dates.

It is important not to purchase any tickets until you are sure you have a firm exchange agreement. Bookings are usually held at no cost until a date specified by the airline when a deposit or full payment must be paid. It is important to communicate with your exchange partners before you confirm anything. Some flexibility will inevitably be required.

Once you have paid for your tickets, send a copy of the tickets or the itinerary to your exchange partners as added security and documentation for them.

HOME EXCHANGE AGREEMENT FORM

Table 7 shows a form which you may duplicate to document any arrangements made with your exchange partners. Send a signed copy to your exchange partners and ask them to sign and return it to you.

This can also be lodged with your home exchange club giving them a record of the pending exchange. Members are unlikely to jeopardise future membership with their chosen club by behaving poorly, so the more documentation you have the better.

Remember now that you have agreed on an exchange, backing out will cause considerable inconvenience, disappointment and financial hardship to your exchange partners. Exchange etiquette demands that you honour your agreement.

Table 7. Home Exchange Agreement Form

HOME EXCHANGE AGREEMENT

I/We, _____ , of _____

_____ have agreed to a home exchange

with _____ , of _____

_____ for a period of _____ weeks/months

from _____ until _____ 20__ inclusive.

No. of adults: ___   No. of children: ___   Ages of children: _____

I/We understand my/our obligations in accepting this home exchange. I/We agree to care for the exchange home in a responsible manner, maintain the property in the state in which it is found and report any damage, breakage or system failure to the designated person. We have agreed to the following terms and conditions with repect to:

a) exchange of keys

_____

_____

b) the payment of utility bills

_____

_____

c) the payment of telephone bills

_____

_____

_____

d) car exchange

_____

_____

_____

_____

e) cleaning/gardening

_____

_____

_____

f) overnight absences from the home/entertainment of overnight guests

_____

_____

_____

g) use and replacement of provisions/food staples

_____

_____

_____

h) security measures

_____

_____

_____

i) minor repairs to household equipment

_____

_____

_____

j) handling of mail

_____

_____

_____

k) use of linens and towels

_____

_____

_____

l) pet care

_____

_____

m) contingency plans

_____

_____

_____

Further, I/we agree to provide each other with the following (delete that which is not applicable):

i   information concerning our respective homes including instructions for the operation of home appliances

ii   names and contact details of trades people to be used in case of system breakdown or emergency

iii   contact details of the designated person(s) who can act as decision maker(s) in our absence

iv   adequate space for the storage of personal effects

v   replacement of (where possible), or financial compensation for breakages

vi   comprehensive information concerning home and car insurance

vii   maps, brochures, local information

viii   full instructions concerning pet care

Other: _____

_____

_____

_____

Signed: _____ Date: _____

Signed: _____ Date: _____

Travelling with Children

*T*he main advantage of exchanging homes with families who have babies and children of similar ages to your own is that all the required equipment is readily available. You need not board aircraft struggling with car seats, high chairs, cots, prams, toys and books. Your children will enjoy all the 'new' toys at the exchange home.

If your exchange guests have children of a similar age to your own, they may have friends in the neighbourhood who will provide instant entertainment for your children. The neighbourhood children will be a wonderful source of information for all the local activities and amenities for children.

Not only will their new friends keep them occupied, but your children will have excellent opportunities for learning about children of another culture. They might even learn a new language or brush up on existing skills.

Exchanging with your children also raises the level of responsibility. Ensure that your children are properly supervised at all times in your host's home. On arrival, inspect the property for any existing damage such as cracked windows, broken equipment and carpet stains and report this to the responsible party overseeing your stay.

If your exchange guests have children of their own, there will exist a mutual tolerance and understanding. Nevertheless, exchange children should be encouraged to act in a responsible manner and be respectful of the property of others. Set some house rules for your children such as where they can and cannot eat and drink, what they are allowed to touch and use and which items they may not.

Reimburse the owners if there are any accidental breakages or spills. It is a good idea to plan on employing a professional carpet cleaning service at the end of your stay.

If you don't have children of your own, but you are accepting children into your home, there are several things you can do by way of preparation to both minimise the impact and to assist your incoming guests.

Firstly, compile a list of rules concerning use of such items as sports equipment, VCR and computer equipment. Clearly state any off-limits areas or items. During the course of your correspondence with your guests you can explain that, along with a list of local amenities and activities for children you are preparing this list of 'do's and don'ts'. Responsible parents will have no objection to this.

Your list of activities for children might include information on neighbourhood activities, memberships to clubs, location of playgrounds, picnic facilities, parks, bike trails and museums.

You can also endeavour to provide equipment for their needs. Ask your guests what equipment they may be likely to require. These items might include a car seat, high chair, cot or playpen. You are not expected to purchase anything on behalf of your guests, but you may be able to borrow such items from family or friends. Alternatively, you could look into hire costs and let your exchange guests know the related expenses.

Pack away any breakables and items that you think might be likely targets.

Bob and Joyce, a retired couple from Oxfordshire accepted an exchange with a couple who had two very young children. Joyce explains how they prepared for it.

"As the swap was for a period of nearly twelve months, we wanted to clear out as many of our belongings as possible to provide adequate space for our guests. We boxed up our personal papers and many of our special things and put them up in the loft. This also took care of the potential problem of small children damaging our belongings.

Our exchange partners were of a similar age to our own daughter who we left in charge of our affairs. As our daughter has children, she was able to assist our guests with events and activities for families. They became very good friends over the ten month exchange and we didn't have any problems at our house at all."

Case Study

Cynthia and Brian live in Wanaka, New Zealand. They exchanged homes with Pam and John from Perth, Australia. The couples arranged their exchange through the electronic and printed directory services of *Latitudes Home Exchange.* Cynthia and Brian had re-subscribed to the printed catalogue service following a couple of successful, prior exchange experiences through the company.

Pam and John, first-time exchangers, joined the electronic service via the web site on the internet. Using their membership password, they were able to access the complete printed directory without actually subscribing to it. They had wanted to visit New Zealand's South Island for some time and were pleasantly surprised when what appeared to be the perfect exchange scenario was readily available to them.

The following shows their respective listings.

John and Pam ********	** **** ****	2 adults	**PERTH**
*** ********** Avenue	** **** ****	2 persons	
Wembley Downs		hmx	house 3bd/2ba
Western Australia 6018			

Biography: Retired couple, 60s, non-smokers

Modern, purpose-built, two-storey brick home close to Perth's beautiful northern beaches. Owners can arrange guest golf passes and loan golf equipment. Close to restaurants, library, shopping, golf courses. Spacious living areas, all modern conveniences, comfortably furnished, garage, off-street parking. 1993 Mitsubishi Magna available. We can also offer B&B for up to two adults – possibly where your arranged exchange overlaps for a night or two and you need temporary additional accommodation. No children.

Destination: NEW ZEALAND (South Island)
flexible length   **flexible dates**   **LT-991-AU-1214**

Brian and Cynthia ******** *** ********** Court Wanaka Central Otago	** **** **** ** **** ****	2 adults 6 persons hmx, hpx	**WANAKA** Dunedin – 3 hr house, 200sm, 4bd/3ba

Biography: Retired, 60s, non-smokers, exp exch

Modern, two-storey home, built to take guests with two double bedrooms downstairs with adjoining bathroom. Main bedroom, with bathroom, upstairs. Wanaka is a small resort centre for all summer outdoor activities including boating, hiking and fishing, and for skiing in winter with two ski-fields within 20 min drive. Queenstown – a major ski resort and tourist centre – is one hour away. There are seven golf courses within range, most with spectacular views. Usual domestic facilities plus wood buring fire (plus wood) for winter. Car exchange offered – 1995 Subaru 4WD – plus garaging. Preferably no children.

Destination: **AUSTRALIA (beach resort esp. Perth), CANADA (Vancouver Isle, flexible)**
flexible length   Oct (Aus); Apr (Can)   LT-001-NZ-5024

Pam and John made contact with Cynthia and Brian by fax as no email address was provided. Cynthia and Brian were away on an exchange in France at the time but wrote back giving a favourable response and the two couples were soon proposing dates and timeframes.

During the negotiations, Brian became ill and the couples were forced to suspend travel plans until the matter was resolved. They decided to put the exchange 'on hold', with the New Zealanders agreeing to advise if and when Brian recovered sufficiently to travel overseas.

Approximately one year passed after the initial contact had been made. Brian's health had improved and the Perth couple had been kept informed on his progress and doctors' recommendations. As soon as he was given the 'all clear', correspondence was resumed and dates were again proposed.

There still remained a period of eight months to arrange all the details before the intended departure. With Brian's health in mind, Pam and John took out insurance coverage against unforeseen circumstances which might force them to cancel the trip.

The couples, of similar ages and backgrounds, immediately began to feel that they were well-matched, and that they had similar tastes in furnishings.

The exchange was a huge success for both couples. Each couple was met at the respective airport by the other couple's daughter and taken to the exchange home to be shown the ropes. The couples knew they would meet at the airport at the start of the exchange. Due to delays in customs, the meeting turned out to be nothing more than a fleeting 'hello and goodbye'.

Cynthia and Brian used a phone card for their calls while Pam and John used the phone and left a list of calls with re-imbursement money. Each couple paid the utility bills at their own home. They used each other's food staples with no particular replacement stipulation. Pam and John have no lawns and Cynthia and Brian's lawns were maintained by friends during the exchange.

As an added bonus, Cynthia and Brian were able to make use of a holiday home owned by Pam and John's son. The house is located in Busselton, about three hours drive south of Perth.

At the end of the exchange, Pam and John returned to Perth a few days before the others were due to leave and spent those nights with their daughter who lives close by. They were able to meet Cynthia and Brian and swap holiday stories. Next year, Cynthia and Brian are expecting a visit from friends of Pam and John whom they met while in Perth.

Pam and John estimated that the month-long exchange saved them AU$7,000 in accommodation, car hire and restaurant meals. But Pam adds, *"The real benefit was having all the comforts of home and a base from which to tour around. The effort is definitely worth it, not that there was really a lot to do.*

Before the exchange, I was concerned about cleaning aspects. I had arranged for cleaners at our home if Cynthia wanted to use them and I would have paid for them on our return. Their grand-daughter was available to do our cleaning if necessary. As it turned out, I needn't have worried. Our home was left in perfect condition.

We also overcame our initial concerns about the use of our car. In fact, we got the better car in the exchange and we encouraged each other to make full use of the vehicles. Being over 55 years, we would have had to pay an excess fee of $400 if we were the 'at-fault' drivers in an accident. Our insurer had no such stipulation if the situation were reversed.

We toured the South Island extensively. The mountains and lakes were so scenic particularly as they were snow covered during our stay."

So what makes a good home swapper? Pam and John say: *"Flexibility. Consideration of the other couple exactly as you would wish them to consider you."*

What follows are the actual letters, faxes and calls exchanged between the two couples to show how their plans evolved. The correspondence illustrates the friendly ease with which they negotiated all the aspects of their exchange.

---

16 March   ***FAX***

Dear John and Pam,

Six months have passed by with Brian's treatment finished in the meantime. Waiting for a small operation and then we feel we will be able to travel again, hopefully in late October.

I am forwarding by mail some places of interest in Wanaka and surrounding districts. Let us know what your plans are and if you are still interested in coming to this part of New Zealand.

Kind regards,

Cynthia and Brian

20 March **TELEPHONE**

Pam phoned back to speak to Cynthia and discuss the dates. Four weeks in October was agreed.

2 April **MAIL**

Dear Cynthia and Brian,

Enclosed is the long promised photo of our house along with some others I took the other day showing our living areas.

After receiving your fax and talking to you on the phone, we started to realise there are quite a lot of things Pam and I will need to get done over the time up to when we actually leave Perth. As we are total novices at this home exchange business, we've made a quick and probably incomplete list of the things that immediately come to mind and have enclosed a copy of it for your info and as perhaps a starting point for matters we will need to think about over the next few months.

We are pretty flexible and are sure that any uncertainties you might have can be easily resolved and would welcome your comments and suggestions on any points you think may need to be discussed.

Travel
Passports
Travel dates and times
Airport transportation

House
Insurance
Household items requiring special care
Utility bill obligations
Telephone obligations
Cleaning

Car
Description
Insurance
Service requirements
Discuss excess costs/additional premium costs
RAC

General
List contacts
Keys
Newspapers
Rubbish collection
Neighbours

John and Pam

30 April   MAIL

Dear Cynthia and Brian,

Thank you so much for the photographs. Your house looks lovely, my colours, that surely must be an indication that we would be compatible couples.

The information on activities available in Wanaka is staggering – we can't compete with that but as John has indicated, we are only 15 minutes walk to the beach and by car you could choose several beaches to go to – all within 25 minutes. The local shopping centre has a nice coffee shop, together with the normal supermarket, chemist, dress shop, florist, Chinese restaurant, hairdresser, etc. There is a public golf course 5 minutes away by car, heated swimming pool nearby but tourist type things are further.

Wine Tours in the Swan Valley are approx. 20 km by car or there are boat tours which are very popular. Rottnest Island is about a one hour ferry ride away and is very popular with beautiful beaches. The city of Fremantle is a very interesting place to visit, a lot of convict-built buildings. It has a cosmopolitan atmosphere with Al Fresco cafes and markets. Perth city is compact and has entertainment venues such as Concert Hall, His Majesty's Theatre and Entertainment Centre. There is also a casino.

Karrinyup shopping centre is about 15 minutes away by car and is very comprehensive.

I am enclosing a photo of ourselves at the front of the house which, incidentally, is situated behind our original house which we sold after 34 years, building this one on 500 square metres. All our neighbours are extremely nice and would be available if you needed help or advice.

Regards,

Pam

12 May   *FAX*

Dear Pam and John,

Many thanks for the photos and letter. Brian has had his operation and everything is working well. He has to go back to the hospital on 30 May and then we hope to be able to make our dates for travel to Perth.

Once this is behind us, we will think of all the things we have to sort out regarding the house and car, etc.

The weather has turned cooler now with snow on the mountains. I don't think Brian will be skiing much with 6 weeks of recuperation required; he might be forced to ski the second slope with me!

You will have to visit the mountain when you are here as it's only a half hour to either ski field. Even if you don't ski, there is lots to see and a lovely café. We are looking forward to exploring your area. You will enjoy our golf course with its marvellous views.

We have a son and family living in Wanaka with three children ages 18, 16 and 14 and they will help with anything you want to know.

Our street is mainly holiday homes, it's lovely as you have the street to yourself except for the holidays and ski season when the population of Wanaka grows from 3,500 to 30,000!

Our daughter lives in Cromwell half an hour away and half an hour to Queenstown so we will probably get her to meet you if you fly into Queenstown airport.

There are so many things to think of but at least we will have something to keep us going and it's all so exciting to visit a new area.

We have plenty of friends who will look after you while you are here, there is a great community spirit amongst us all, so many people have moved here for retirement.

We will write again after the next visit to hospital which is 3.5 hours away, another place you will have to visit!

Regards,

Cynthia and Brian

3 Jun   MAIL

Dear Pam and John,

Enclosed are the photos of the inside of some of the rooms. The bathrooms are missing and the room above the downstairs bedrooms which is what Brian calls my junk room (typewriter, ironing board, sewing machine, bed settee which can be used for extra guests).

Brian has to return to clinic in 2 weeks and the surgeon will make a decision on whether an operation is necessary. We are hoping the pills he is on will do the trick.

The snow came while we were away in Dunedin and looks beautiful on the mountain with a lovely sunny day, must take some more photos.

As soon as we know what is happening we will contact you re: booking and all the other details.

Will enclose another booklet which might give you more idea of other places you could visit.

Regards,

Cynthia and Brian

16 Jun   FAX

Dear Pam and John,

We have only one more visit to the surgeon to clear Brian for golf again.

We are starting to enquire about flights and about going to Melbourne to and from Perth. We have quite a few frequent flyer points to use up so we will see what is available for early October and will fax you before we confirm anything.

You could fly into Christchurch and travel to Wanaka by bus but if you connect from Christchurch to Queenstown by plane, we will be able to have you picked up in Queenstown.

House insurance will be covered; can't say there is anything in the house requiring special care; we would pay for what you use in electricity and the usual telephone bill. If the phone was used for international calls or toll calls within New Zealand, they would be at your cost. We have a calling card that we use outside New Zealand which is charged to our account.

Cleaning: My grand daughter would clean if needed and I would pay her.

Car: 1995 4WD Subaru Legacy Station wagon. It is covered for other drivers. Brian was service manager for BMW and Holden with a GM franchise in Dunedin and our son, who lives in Wanaka, is a trained motor mechanic now in charge of a bus fleet. You shouldn't have any problem with the car but you could contact Gavin. The vehicle will be serviced prior to your arrival. We have full insurance on the car. If you were at fault in an accident, the excess (deductible) for overseas drivers is NZ$400.

We will leave a list of contact people in case of problems i.e. plumber, electrician and details of the rubbish collection, etc.

We had a good fall of snow last week and the ski season starts on 25 June; the mountains look beautiful even if it is cold some days.

Looking forward to hearing from you again.

Regards,

Cynthia and Brian

18 Jun   *FAX*

Dear Cynthia and Brian,

Thanks for your letter of 3 June. It's really good news to hear that Brian is well on the way to recovery.

The similarity between our houses, curtain types, etc. is remarkable and I'm sure you will find our place easy to fit into and vice versa.

When you know your flight booking dates we will go ahead with ours to coincide as closely as possible. Our daughter Vicki will meet you at the airport – it's about a 45 minute drive.

At this stage we are planning on flying to Queenstown but if you think we would be better bussing it from Christchurch we would take your advice.

About insurance, telephone, car etc. mentioned in your letter – suits us fine and we will do the same for you.

Pam will be writing to you about any domestic things which come to mind once we have dates arranged. In the meantime I will get some brochures and post them to you.

We are both looking forward very much to our New Zealand holiday and depending on how flight dates work out it might happen that we will meet you both if there is an overlap.

Regards,

John

3 July *FAX*

Dear Pam and John,

Flying direct Auckland to Perth NZ113, Monday 25 Sept arriving Perth 6.40 pm. Departing Perth NZ114 Weds 25 October, 8 pm. How will this suit you? We have till 10 July to change flights. This was the only flight we could get to use our frequent flyer points. Tried to fly to Sydney and on to Perth but the dates didn't work. Now have to fly from Christchurch to Auckland or drive to Auckland. We are not worrying about this part of the journey till later.

Cold day today, need more snow as most of it has melted. Will ring you tonight to confirm if everything is okay with you for these dates.

Regards,

Cynthia and Brian

5 July *FAX*

Dear Cynthia and Brian,

We have managed to book flights on Air New Zealand flight NZ639 as follows:
Depart Perth Monday 25 September, 8 pm
Arrive Queenstown Tuesday 26 September, 11.50 am.

Your flight arrives in Perth at 6.40 pm on Monday and we will be able to meet you at the airport with our daughter Vicki, before we depart at 8.00 pm.

Our return flight arrives in Perth International on Monday 23 October at 6.40 pm but we will get Vicki to pick us up and we will stay with her Monday and Tuesday. This flight will give us the opportunity of taking you out to the airport on Wednesday and possibly seeing you before that if you have some free time. We will be in touch again shortly.

Pam and John

18 July   **FAX**

Dear Pam and John,

Received your time of arrival and our daughter Wendy will meet you in her car and bring you to Wanaka. She lives at Cromwell which is between Wanaka and Queenstown.

So I'm now cleaning up places that I haven't looked at for a while – a good winter's day job. It's low cloud here in Wanaka but up the mountain is brilliant sunshine. We had a lovely day there yesterday skiing with friends and will go back again tomorrow.

Have organised another trip to Dunedin for Brian to see the surgeon before we leave.

We haven't had any more snow but they are predicting it for the next month and there should be plenty when you arrive here. You will enjoy a trip to the Cardrona ski field where we go. Hope you like heights and mountain roads. We haven't had to use chains very often as the Subaru handles the conditions well.

Still have to book our flights from Christchurch to Auckland and return; will go there a few days before our departure as I have a sister there and Brian has a brother who we will stay with. Coming home we will probably also stay over for a day as we will have the drive home from Christchurch.

I'm really looking forward to some warmer weather in your part of the country.

Regards,

Cynthia and Brian

26 *July*   *FAX*

Dear Cynthia and Brian,

Thanks for your fax of the 18th. We have booked and paid for our fares and are sending our itinerary with this note. You will notice our departure date from Queenstown is the 23 Oct – we will be staying with our daughter (she lives quite close by) for the two days until you leave Perth and maybe we can arrange to go out with you during that time.

Passports have been renewed and we are now starting to get to the impatient to get there stage even though it's a couple of months to go.

Wanaka with its ski fields and other attractions we've been told about by friends seems to be the place in New Zealand to spend time. We will certainly be having a good look around during our time there and hope you will be doing the same over here.

It will be the wildflower season down in the south west when you are in Perth and the area is well worth visiting. It's also where the forests and vineyards with wine tasting and restaurants are.

Along the coast in that area south from about Busselton, there are some well known and popular beaches but we also have those nearby in Perth.

A really good trip to consider is a drive over a few days along the southwest coast down to Albany – it could be a bit longer than you may want but your time away could be varied to suit, i.e. come home early or extend depending how you feel.

We will have a map of the Perth area with places marked on it that we think you would like to see – beaches, shopping centres, markets etc. and Vicki our daughter or our neighbours and others will be on hand if you need help.

Up until three days ago, we have had a fair bit of much needed rain but it's now fine and clear with max temps in the 18 to 20°C range.

Winter will soon be over and it should be into one of the best times of the year when you are here with probably a bit of body surfing weather towards the middle of October.

All the best,

John and Pam

3 August **FAX**

Dear Pam and John,

What a hassle trying to use frequent flyer points – you get so far then you can't co-ordinate the next flight. I'm waiting for more points to be credited to our account so we can fly from Auckland direct to Perth. The date would be 25 September. We can get from Christchurch to Melbourne but the dates don't fit in so we may have to revert to booking a normal flight and use the points to upgrade.

It will be better if you fly into Queenstown as it's a six hour bus trip from Christchurch to Wanaka.

Have had two days skiing, wonderful snow and weather. Brian is back at golf today.

I'll ring or fax as soon as I can sort all this out.

Regards,

Cynthia

8 August **MAIL**

Dear Pam and John,

Everything in order at this end, all flights booked, leave possibly Wed 20 and drive to Christchurch, staying a couple of days and then flying to Auckland for the weekend before leaving for Perth on the following Monday. Coming back, we will stay in Auckland two nights and Christchurch one night before driving home again.

You need not bring a warm jacket as our ski jackets are in the wardrobe if it's that cold. It's warmer during the day now and lighter at night, you will still have to light the fire for warmth in the evening.

We will do a trip away over there and guess you will do several over here, especially down to Milford Sound where you would be best to stay at Te Anau. A trip to Dunedin or Christchurch would be worthwhile also.

I will send this so I can include a photo of Wendy so you can recognise her at the airport.

Really looking forward to this holiday and exchange. You don't have to stay with your daughter on return if you want to come home, we don't mind, after all it's your house.

Regards,

Cynthia and Brian

15 August   **EMAIL**

Hello Pam and John,

This is Ian and Sally, friends of Cynthia and Brian. We look forward to meeting you here in Wanaka. Please feel free to send messages here for Cynthia and Brian or for yourselves later.

Cheers for now,

Ian and Sally

4 September   *FAX*

Dear Cynthia and Brian,

Well we are close to countdown now and I was finalising the car insurance, when I discovered that the insurance company requires your dates of birth and accident history over the past 12 months. No official documentation is required.

Our Policy allows us the first accident of the policy year free of charge with subsequent accidents incurring a penalty of $200–$300 for loss of No Claim Bonus.

Thanks for the offer to stay when we return but we are happy to go to Vicki's. We will definitely contact you on the 24th.

Looking forward to meeting you at the airport.

Regards,

Pam

4 September **FAX**

Dear Pam and John,

Received your fax. Our dates of birth are Cynthia: 29/3/36; Brian: 7/4/34. No accidents in the last 12 months.

Just home from the hospital where Brian had his check-up. All's well so we can really look forward to our holiday now. We have nobody coming over to join us, most have had their holidays this year.

Temperatures have become warmer, 13-15 °C during the day. Bulbs are coming out in the gardens, spring I think has arrived.

We will fax you before we leave on the 20th.

Regards,

Cynthia and Brian

14 September **FAX**

Dear Pam and John,

Just off the ski field, glorious snow, won't be able to go again. On Wednesday we leave for Christchurch.

Hope to see you at the airport but with you leaving on our inbound flight, we wonder if there will be enough time for us to get through customs before you leave.

Wendy has your time of arrival and will be there to meet you. If there are any delays, you have all the phone numbers. It will be a long trip for you.

We've packed our swimming gear and hope it's warm enough for us to swim. We are looking forward to coming. I'm sure we are going to enjoy it all and you will enjoy it here.

Cheers from the skiers of Wanaka,

Cynthia and Brian

The following shows the list of instructions left by Pam and John for their daughter Vicki who was appointed to oversee the incoming guests.

NOTES FOR VICKI

Contact details:
NZ telephone number: 0011 643 000 0000
NZ fax number: 0015 643 000 0000

Mail arrangements:
Could you phone Cynthia and Brian once a week and ask if there is any mail for us. If there are bills or letters, would you be able to collect them, open them and if necessary let us know if we need to do anything.

Neighbour Joy will collect our mail if they go away.

We will leave the cellar key with you. Our personal papers including cheque books and wills are in there should you need them.

Passport numbers:
Pam N0000000
John M0000000

Table 8 shows Pam and John's information sheet left for Cynthia and Brian.

Table 8. Sample Information Sheet

INFORMATION WHICH MIGHT BE USEFUL

BioMax drainage system – located in lower corner of the back outside area. This is our drainage system which is in fact a mini sewage farm. You don't have to do anything different. The only thing you will notice is that the 'reticulation' goes on shortly after you have used any water. This is because all the water we use goes down the drains into an aerobic/anaerobic processor, is purified and pumped onto the garden as fresh water.

There is an alarm system for it in the laundry and, in the unlikely event of a problem, see the fault list attached. The phone number for service is 00000000, code 00000 (answering service).

Garbage bin – located under the hot water service near the back verandah on the lower level paved area and should be placed on the edge of the front lawn (handles to the rear so the truck can pick it up) on Monday evenings for collection on Tuesdays between 7 and 10 am.

Watering
Would you mind watering the few pots around the place as necessary and turn the timer on for the garden along the drive fence (45-60 min). It is an under surface trickle system.

Work shed
Use any tools you need.

Security
For insurance purposes, we make sure the house is secured with doors and windows locked when we go out. The under stairs cellar has personal papers locked in it.

Insurance
House and Contents:
Insurance company – Corporate Home Unit – Tel: 9123 4567
Policy number: 0000000
Car insurance:
Insurance company – GIO – Tel: 9123 4567
Policy number: 0000000

RAC card
Car is covered by RAC who will attend breakdowns in the city and country.

Keys
Vicki has spares of all keys and there are two sets for you.

Phone numbers
House cleaner _____

Doctor _____

Mechanic _____

Electrician _____

Vicki (our daughter)   _____

Bruce (our son)   _____

This house   _____

Papers
The Australian (national) is delivered each Tuesday, Thursday and Saturday at the top of the drive and Joy from No. 15 usually drops her West Australian (local) for Wednesday and Saturday after she has read them. The Thursday Australian has the TV program info. If you don't want the delivery to continue, the number is 9123 4567.

Pantry/fridge
Help yourselves

Stove
Normal operation but keep oven door open when using griller. John didn't once, with frightening results!

Bessamer ware (Black Cookware)
To protect the Teflon surfaces, use only the black utensils located in the white bench for this cookware.

Cutlery
Table cutlery is in the dresser drawer. We have found that the dishwasher detergent corrodes the knives where the handle and blade join and would appreciate it if you would wash them separately.

Washing machine
Program has been set to favourite but can be changed easily per instruction booklet.

Dishwasher
Pre-set. Press 'power' and 'start'. See booklet if you want to change it. Dishwasher powder detergent is placed in the right-hand side cup of the dispenser on the inside of the machine door. Close dispenser lid.

Bread machine
It takes only a few minutes to load the pre-mixed flour, water and yeast and you can have fresh bread daily. Instructions are on the machine in the laundry and there is a booklet with different recipes.

Microwave
Normal operation

BBQ
Located outside on the lounge side of the house. On castors; for convenience, John wheels it to the French doors when cooking.

TV
Stations/channels are 2, 5, 7, 9 and 10. Use the skip button for convenience in changing channels. Channel one button switches in the VCR.

Video
Old but good. Repaired and serviced recently. Instruction book with it.

Air-conditioner
Used for heating and cooling. Remote control is self-explanatory. Press the silver button at the bottom of the handpiece to start and stop. The top button is for pre-setting and it is a nuisance trying to disengage it.

Neighbours
George and Kirsten: No 11
Joy: No 15
Heather: No 13
They know who you are and will make contact with you.

Mail
Vicki will phone you to check and call in to collect our mail. If you go away, Joy from No. 15 will check and collect it.

Entertainment Book
Lists restaurants and entertainment available to us (and now you) at discount prices. Please feel free to use the coupons.

Maps
We have made a large map in the computer room which has places of interest marked on it for you. Maps of Western Australia are with the tourist brochures. There's a street map under the passenger seat in the car. George (No 11) will point you in the right direction if you want suggestions on trips and can help with general queries.

Golf
Clubs are in the garage, see street maps book for public course. If you would like a game at our club, Seaview Golf Club in Cottesloe, phone Alma, 9123 4567.

Enjoy!

Preparing Your Home and Car for Your Exchange Guests

"We had a nice surprise when we arrived at the Canadian home. Everything was just perfect like in 'The Darling Buds Of May'."

Sid and Sylvia J., Strathmore, Victoria

It is now time to prepare your home and car for your arriving guests.

The first step is the compilation of an information file. The purpose of this file is to specify details surrounding the topics already discussed with your exchange partners. It provides very specific information about the running of your home such as instructions on operating the security system.

The file also provides useful information to help your guests settle into their new environment such as letting them know where best to shop and eat out locally and how to use the public transport system.

Preparing the information file will not only serve as an invaluable resource for your guests on arrival and during their stay but will also prompt you to organise the tasks you need to undertake in preparing your home.

The second step comprises the physical preparation of your home and making your guests feel welcome. The items covered in this stage of the home exchange process are:

Compiling an information file
Making your guests feel welcome

House-keeping

Sentimental or valuable items

Linens and towels

Preparing your car

Pets

Preparing a second home

Provisions for an exchange series

COMPILING AN INFORMATION FILE

This may take some thought and time to put together but it will be much appreciated by your exchange guests and, once prepared, it will be ready for all your subsequent exchanges. It is time well spent because it could help determine how well your property is looked after.

Leave explanations regarding operation of appliances, security systems and air-conditioning units. Supply all the manuals, as manufacturers' handbooks are a good source of information.

The most common baffling appliance appears to be the microwave. It is worth noting that many exchangers have reported finding other appliances such as video recorders and even cooking stoves totally unfathomable. Cynthia of Wanaka commented: *"We wiped off the first few messages on the answering machine because we just couldn't work out how to use it."*

List the emergency numbers or post them near the telephone. These vary from country to country, so don't assume they will be known. Provide the name and contact details of someone you have appointed to make decisions regarding your home.

In case of an emergency, you will know the whereabouts of the home owners – they should be at your house. However, they may be touring the environs, so make sure that there's a contact person appointed.

Indicate which day the rubbish is collected and list any special procedures such as re-cycling.

Outline any gardening and pool maintenance or irrigation procedures that will be expected. If your guests cannot accept gardening duties, make alternative arrangements for lawn mowing and gardening services. If there are house plants requiring attention, explain what is required.

Give the location of the power and water shut-offs for emergencies.

Explain how the public transport system works in your area and where it can be boarded. Many people prefer to use public transport around the cities but things that seem quite obvious to locals, such as how and where to purchase a train ticket, can prove a baffling prospect for international visitors. Leave specific information about the coins required, how to purchase rail tickets, train and bus schedules and explain where the bus stops. If you don't use public transport yourself, leave your guests some instructions on where the information can be obtained.

Table 9. Fact File for Exchange Guests

FACT FILE FOR EXCHANGE GUESTS RESIDING AT: _____

_____

A. Contact people:

Primary person to be contacted in our absence

Name: _____ Telephone: _____

Person to be contacted in an emergency

Name: _____ Telephone: _____

Persons responsible for house/pet/car in our absence

Name: _____ Telephone: _____

Name: _____ Telephone: _____

Neighbours and friends

Name(s): _____ Telephone: _____

Address: _____

Name(s): _____ Telephone: _____

Address: _____

Name(s): _____ Telephone: _____

Address: _____

Baby-sitters

Name: _____ Telephone: _____

Cost per hour: _____ Availability: _____

Age: _____ Notes: _____

Name: _____   Telephone: _____

Cost per hour: _____   Availability: _____

Age: _____   Notes: _____

B. Emergency phone numbers:

Ambulance: _____   Fire department: _____   Police: _____

Local doctor

Name: _____   Telephone: _____

Address: _____

Local dentist

Name: _____   Telephone: _____

Address: _____

Local hospital or emergency department

Name: _____   Telephone: _____

Address: _____

C. General information:

Taxi service

Name: _____   Telephone: _____

Plumber

Name: _____   Telephone: _____

Electrician

Name: _____   Telephone: _____

Carpet cleaner

Name: _____ Telephone: _____

General repair places

For repair of: _____

Name: _____ Telephone: _____

For repair of: _____

Name: _____ Telephone: _____

Appliance repairs

For repair of: _____

Name: _____ Telephone: _____

For repair of: _____

Name: _____ Telephone: _____

D. Supply shut-offs/mains:

Gas shut-off

Located: _____

Water shut-off

Located: _____

Fuse box

Located: _____

E. Instructions for:

Re-cycling _____

Rubbish collection _____

_____

Deliveries _____

_____

F. Recreational and general facilities:

Local shops

Directions: _____

_____

Nearest recommended shopping mall

Directions: _____

_____

Banks

Directions: _____

_____

Post office

Directions: _____

_____

G. Our favourite restaurants and takeaways:

Name: _____   Type of food: _____

Price range: _____   Closed: _____

Directions: _____

Name: _____ Type of food: _____

Price range: _____ Closed: _____

Directions: _____

Name: _____ Type of food: _____

Price range: _____ Closed: _____

Directions: _____

H. Tourist information:

Checklist:

    List of attractions, tours and special places to visit with directions

    Maps with places marked on it such as shops, markets, etc.

    Leave your dine-out book

    Provide travel tips

I. Car information:

Checklist:

    Insurance papers

    Registration details

    Letter giving guests permission to drive your car

    Owner's manual

Instructions for quirks of our vehicle: _____

_____

Fuel requirements: _____

Repair and service

Name: _____   Telephone: _____

Address: _____

Parking/garaging instructions: _____

_____

Your fact file might include some or all of the details in Table 9. Items concerning the car can be moved to the glove compartment of the car after they have been reviewed by your guests.

The author's permission is granted to copy and use Table 9 for the sole purpose of arranging a personal home exchange.

Bob and Joy from Launceston leave the following instruction sheet for their guests (Table 10).

Table 10. Sample Instruction Sheet

Dear _____ ,

Welcome to your new temporary home. Please feel free to consider this dwelling and its contents 'yours' for the period you are here. Some house-keeping notes may help you:

Keys/Security

The remote control for the roller door is kept in the car. There is also a manual button on the motor unit itself. Our practice when leaving has been to deadlock all external doors and slip the barrel bolts on the downstairs unit and laundry doors. House and contents insurance policy is with Colin.

Microwave and fan-forced oven

Standard operating procedure. Manuals are in the bottom drawer beneath the oven.

Fridge

Automatic defrost. Shouldn't need any attention.

Dishwasher

Before turning cycle selection knob, ensure the power buttons are OFF. Set the cycle desired (please operate on cycle 3, 4 or 6 only). Then press the power button to commence the cycle selected.

Provisioning

In the garden, you'll find carrots, pumpkin, parsnip, cos lettuce and lemons. Help yourself to these but we would ask that you replenish other consumables if you choose to use them from pantry stocks.

Linen/blankets

All beds have electric blankets fitted. Additional blankets and pillows, spare linen, sheets, towels, etc. are in the hallway linen press.

Washing machine

Fully automatic. Load clothes. Place detergent in the drawer, close the lid and press power (back top right). Machine is currently set for cold water washing. If you wish to use that setting, press start 'fuzzy' button (bottom right). Machine automatically fills to the level it determines (based on amount of clothing it senses) and completes the cycle. When finished, it turns itself off and beeps several times to tell you so. Occasionally, if the load becomes unbalanced during a cycle, it will beep to ask you to re-position the load evenly. Having done so, it will restart automatically.

TV/video

There are four channels for TV. ABC is 3; SBS 4; WIN 6 and Southern Cross 9. The TV is set to operate through the video player as follows:

- Press power button on NEC (smaller of the two) remote. This gives picture and sound. Volume controls are on that control (mute doesn't work!).

- To change channels, use the Mitsubishi (larger) remote. Press the figure for the channel you require.

- To record a program, ensure video is in player, press 'rec' on the large remote. To play video, insert cassette, press 'play'.

- To tape a program on one channel whilst watching another, start the TV on the channel to be taped and commence taping. Then using the small remote control, press the number of the channel you wish to watch. On the larger remote, press 'TV/video'. Note that the sound on channel 9 when using this system is periodically scratchy. To return to normal, simply reverse the procedure. Press 'TV/video' (large console), press '1' on the small console, press 'stop' on the large console. Rewind taped video.

Heating

The wood heater is able to heat all upstairs and has a 3-speed fan, though we hardly ever need it. Switch is at bottom right-hand side of heater. Wood is plentiful and starting sticks are provided. There is an axe at the wood pile if you need more. The damper on the heater is open when at the extreme right-hand position. The downstairs unit has an electric heater.

Motor car

Automatic 3-litre Mitsubishi Sports. Unleaded fuel. Tank will be full on delivery and should be full when handed back. Comprehensive insurance policy is with AAMI who have been advised that you are authorised to drive the vehicle. There is a standard excess of $275 which is the driver's responsibility. This is waived by the insurer if the 'at fault' driver can be identified to them. Policy number is 012 345 678.

Maintenance

You'll find an iron, vacuum cleaner, brooms, etc. in the laundry cupboard. Hand tools, etc. are kept in the workshop off the garage.

Emergency

My brother, Bruce, lives a couple of minutes away at _____. He has a complete set of spare keys and has my authority to deal with any matter requiring decision. Don't be afraid to seek his help if you need it. Norman has back-up authority.

External

Lawns will be mown once or twice according to need. Garden is largely dormant now, feel free to help yourself to any produce from the soil. Refuse and rubbish is collected from the road verge early on Wednesdays. Bin is kept in the carport area.

Telephone

The phone has been read. It will be read again on your departure and the account forwarded to you.

Important numbers

Emergency: <u>000</u>

This house: _____

Local police: _____

General hospital: _____

Norman: _____

Bruce: _____

Colin: _____

MAKING YOUR GUESTS FEEL WELCOME

You may like to leave a small grocery pack in the fridge comprising essential food staples to welcome your guests. The fridge should otherwise be cleaned out.

Provide a library card. Make arrangements for your guests to make use of facilities that you enjoy – tennis club, gym, seniors' activities, etc.

Leave copies of recent local and regional papers. These will prove a good resource for your guests.

Leave your exchange guests a copy of *Who's Been Sleeping In My Bed?*. If you've both read the information, it will help to unite your philosophy on home swapping.

If your guests are coming from another country, leave some spare change in your local currency. This will be especially helpful if they arrive over a weekend.

Arrange for some hospitality from your family or neighbours; this usually becomes the highlight of the trip. Perhaps your friends or relatives can take your guests under their wing for a day or so. This will afford you some feedback about the occupants especially if you were unable to meet prior to the exchange.

If you have accepted small children, ensure that poisons, medicines and cleaning materials are securely locked out of reach.

Provide a reasonable amount of cupboard space for your guests' belongings in the bathroom and bedrooms. Remove personal items from dresser tops and items that require constant dusting such as photo frames.

Some participants draw up an inventory of items and request that this be checked and signed within a few days of arrival. This can be given to a responsible neighbour or relative for safe-keeping or mailed to each other. However, remember to extend trust to your exchange guests.

HOUSE-KEEPING

Make sure your house is clean and tidy for your guests. House-keeping standards will vary and you will need to allow for some tolerance in this area. To satisfy everyone's expectations and remove any subjectivity, professional cleaning at the beginning and end of the stay is *strongly recommended*.

It may be that your guests are the better house-keepers and will need to exercise some tolerance on their own part. Very few complaints are lodged against other exchangers, but almost all have to do with cleaning standards.

One report concerned a home not left tidy for the arriving guests. Di and Chris of McLeans Ridge, New South Wales couldn't believe how their Washington, USA exchange partners, a professional couple, lived. *"They made no effort to present their very nice home. We rose above their lack of order and enjoyed ourselves despite them.*

They left our house in reasonable condition but left all their breakfast gear on the table and just walked out! To anyone considering an exchange, we recommend you attempt to gather as much information and as many photos as possible to avoid experiences like this."

On the other hand, Fiona from Perth had this to say about the condition of her home on return: *"Even the windows were cleaned. My parents were taking pictures of our house after they left as they had never seen it look so good. Our pool and garden were in top condition and the fridge and pantry had plenty of food. These were lovely people who took great care of our home and car."* She was referring to her exchange guests from London.

Fiona's findings are fairly typical. John and Valerie filed this report about the condition of their home following their exchange to Horsham, England: *"On returning home, we were so pleased with the cleanliness and the home was as if nobody had been in it at all. Even the car was cleaned and polished."*

Similar findings were expressed by Bob and Joy of Tasmania. *"We have never had any problems with any of our exchanges. In fact, we have always been hard pressed to even know that our home was occupied during our absences, such has been the cleanliness witnessed on our return."*

An independent agent can provide a property condition report. Consider an agreement whereby if the home is not found satisfactory by the guests on arrival, the owner will pay for a professional cleaning service. Make cleaning materials readily available.

SENTIMENTAL OR VALUABLE ITEMS

Consider putting important documents and jewellery in a lock-box at the bank. Don't leave your priceless heirlooms lying around if you have accepted small children. You may wish to pack up some of your more valued items for storage with a relative or use one bedroom for storage. State clearly those areas or items which are off-limits.

LINENS AND TOWELS

It is customary to make readily available enough linens and towels to make your guests comfortable on arrival. Beds should be made up. Travelling overseas with bulky items can be avoided if you agree to allow the use of personal linens.

A common remark following exchanges is that there were not enough linens. Provide at least one change of sheets for each bed and state where extra linens are stored. This will pay off at the end of the exchange when your guests will be able to put clean sheets on the beds in readiness for your own return home.

Some exchangers have offered the use of overcoats and warm clothing where the sizes are compatible.

PREPARING YOUR CAR

Secure a drivers handbook for your guests if the rules in your country are likely to differ from theirs such as is the case between the United States and Commonwealth countries.

It is recommended that each car owner leave a signed notice in the vehicle authorising their exchange partners to use the car. Getting pulled over by the police is no fun anywhere but it can be especially difficult to prove you're legally in possession of a vehicle in a foreign country, especially if no-one seems to be speaking your language.

Indicate where you normally have your repairs and servicing carried out.

Leave plenty of road maps in the car. Leave details of the best places to park in larger towns and cities as this can be daunting to international visitors.

Explain any quirks of the car. Where possible, designate a friend or family member who knows the vehicle well and who has ultimate responsibility in decision-making.

The car should be handed over with a full tank of petrol each time. At the end of use, it should be washed and vacuumed throughout. Ensure it is properly secured and the keys handed over to the designated person.

PETS

Ensure that you leave an adequate supply of pet food and any pet pills to cover your absence. Make sure that collars, leads and 'pooch pouches' are readily available.

PREPARING A SECOND HOME

If you are exchanging a second home, make sure that you have accurately and properly represented it. Think of items that would make your guests more comfortable and try to provide them for their stay. These might include reading material, games and adequate kitchen utensils.

PROVISIONS FOR AN EXCHANGE SERIES

If you have arranged a series of exchanges with various parties, it is a good idea to appoint a responsible party to manage the handover between your respective guests. This person will not only hand over the keys and provide the normal introduction to your home but can also inspect for damage and assess the level of cleanliness after each party vacates.

Professional cleaners are highly recommended following every individual stay because you cannot otherwise guarantee that each of the subsequent exchange guests will find your home in the same condition as you intended. By taking these additional steps, there can be no disputes or shifting blame should something go wrong.

Maintaining and Leaving Your Exchange Home in Good Order

LOOKING AFTER YOUR EXCHANGE HOME

*I*t is important to follow all instructions left by your hosts concerning their home, its contents and the car. Immediately on acceptance of the vehicle, photograph, inspect, document and report to the owner or designated person any visible existing damage.

Make sure that you always properly secure your host's home when not in residence including activating any security systems in place.

Honour your exchange hosts' wishes with respect to any off-limits items or areas – or you could get 'caught out' as Bob of Tasmania explains:

"One of our exchange guests decided she would like to try out the two-person spa. This is located in our third bathroom, one not normally expected to be used by our house guests as they have use of a fully self-contained flat below our main home.

This lady filled up our spa, added some bubble bath, turned on the jets and proceeded to enjoy the ambience – complete with a glass or two of wine.

As we hadn't authorised her to use the facility, we hadn't provided any instructions on its use. It has a three position operation button and she didn't know how to turn it off.

Our neighbours still hoot with laughter when they recall the sight of our embarrassed guest, skimpily clad and covered in bubbles, the effects of the wine clearly visible, knocking on their door seeking help in turning off the spa."

LEAVING YOUR EXCHANGE HOME IN GOOD ORDER

At the end of your stay, you'll want to make sure that your 'home from home' is left exactly as you found it. Employing a professional cleaning company is strongly recommended. As already stressed, house-keeping standards vary considerably and this will remove any subjectivity.

Check through your original agreement to refresh your memory on the arrangements you made with your exchange partners. The dynamics of your relationship with your exchange partners may well have changed since you first made this agreement. Feeling more like friends, you might now be prompted to 'go the extra mile' for them.

Consider cooking a nice meal to welcome them home on their return if the circumstances permit. This can be left in the fridge or freezer. You probably wouldn't feel comfortable 'entertaining' your hosts in their own home so, if there is to be any overlap, you could offer to take them out to a restaurant instead.

Replace any food staples that you've used. If your hosts will be returning home shortly after you leave, a nice gesture is to stock the fridge with milk, cheese, yoghurt, eggs and other perishables. Leave a few basic grocery items to allow them to make themselves breakfast, a sandwich and a drink.

Clean out the fridge because your hosts definitely do not want to come home to your spaghetti leftovers, even though you are the most acclaimed bolognaise chef in your home town.

Where possible, launder any used sheets and towels before you depart. At the very least, beds should be stripped and, if you have to rush off in the very early hours to catch a plane, leave a brief note expressing your regret at being unable to deal with the laundry.

If you have more time, consider doing the laundry and asking a neighbour to take it out of the dryer (or bring it in from the washing line) later in the day. Whatever you decide to do about the laundry, don't leave dirty sheets on the bed for your hosts to deal with. This is really bad form.

Leave money for any breakages that you were unable to replace. Be honest about any damage that might have occurred.

If you've found it necessary to purchase items for the home to make your stay more comfortable, just leave them for your hosts. Future exchangers will probably appreciate it. John and Louvain of Perth became known as the 'frypan exchangers' after they found it necessary to purchase a decent frypan at each of their first three exchange homes. I believe John now packs his own frypan whenever he travels to an exchange home.

If you insist on tackling the cleaning yourselves, the last day or so of your stay needs to be allocated for the task. This depends, in part, on how long you've been in residence and how much cleaning you've done along the way.

If you can remember back to when you were a tenant, pretend you are moving out of a rented property and you want your cleaning deposit returned. Items needing special attention include stove top, oven, microwave, fridge, toilet, bathtub and shower stalls. These are the places where we tend to be less tolerant of 'other people's grime'.

Check the carpets for stains especially if you have young children. Professional carpet cleaners can be found in the phone book and prices are competitive.

Finally, a really nice gesture is to leave your hosts a small gift as a token of your appreciation. An appropriate gift would be a copy of *Who's Been Sleeping In My Bed?*.

When You Arrive Home

*O*ne of the first items of business on your return is to ensure that any unpaid bills are settled. Photocopies of bills can be exchanged and any differences settled.

If you do find items which have been broken or are missing, you should raise this with your guests. Give them a chance to rectify any problems. If the matter isn't easily resolved, state in writing the nature of the problem and exactly what it is you are seeking from them and send it along with a copy to your home exchange club. Knowing that they have been reported will almost certainly lead to a response in your favour. Problems of this nature are very rare and you need to keep things in perspective.

If there is evidence of misconduct, document this and report to the club to whom you subscribed. Hopefully, they will have a system of blacklisting such members.

In most cases, however, there will be no problems and you will find your home and contents in good order.

It is a good idea to write a thank you note to your exchangers. This serves to give some closure to the whole transaction.

Following the completion of your exchange transactions, obtain references from your hosts which can be used for subsequent exchanges. You can now update your own listing and letter of introduction to reflect the fact that you are now 'experienced exchangers'.

If your membership with a formal club has not yet expired, make sure that you update the details of your listing. If you are keen to begin planning your next exchange, change the dates and destinations to reflect your new request. If you have no plans for another exchange, you should ask the club to delete your listing as a courtesy to their other members.

Clubs offering printed directories or electronic services will no doubt be appreciative of the feedback since they typically have no way of keeping track of which members were successful in finding an exchange or how the exchange turned out.

If your exchange was arranged through a custom matching service, you should receive some form of feedback questionnaire shortly after your return. It is important that you take the time complete this so that the club can improve its service and document the outcome of your exchange.

If your club fails to seek your feedback after your exchange, it might be time to look for another company.

Disabled Travellers

*I*f you have a disability, the ability to maintain your usual level of independence will leave you free to enjoy your holiday.

Many home exchange club directories indicate which homes supposedly have disabled access. However, as most of these homes are not actually lived in by wheelchair users, you will need to thoroughly investigate exactly what is meant by 'wheelchair accessible'.

To find an exchange home which meets your specific requirements with respect to accessibility and structural adaptations, it may be preferable to select an organisation whose participants have a person with a disability in the household.

Not only will you have a better understanding of each other's particular requirements for accessibility; but the home will be more likely to have the necessary structural alterations such as ramps and bathroom and kitchen adaptations.

You will also have available some first-hand knowledge of the local resources at your destination.

The following are two organisations which assist disabled travellers with international exchanges.

Mobility International USA (MIUSA)

P.O. Box 10767
Eugene, Oregon USA 97440
Tel: (541) 343 1284   *Fax:* (541) 343 6812

Email: info@miusa.org
http://www.miusa.org/

Mobility International USA (MIUSA) was co-founded in 1981. The mission of MIUSA (a US-based, national non-profit organisation), is to empower people with disabilities around the world through international exchange, information, technical assistance and training and to ensure the inclusion of people with disabilities in international exchange and development programs.

MIUSA, with sponsorship from the Bureau of Educational and Cultural Affairs (ECA) of the U.S. Department of State, manages the National Clearinghouse on Disability and Exchange (NCDE).

The NCDE works to educate people with disabilities and disability-related organisations about international educational exchange opportunities, promoting the inclusion of people with disabilities in all types of exchange, community and volunteer service programs.

NCDE provides free information and referral to individuals with disabilities interested in participating in international programs. It also advises exchange programs on how to accommodate participants with disabilities.

Individuals with disabilities are encouraged to explore the many ways their international interests can be fulfilled through international exchange. NCDE can provide accommodation tips, homestay assessment checklists and contacts overseas to facilitate a successful experience.

Home exchange can be a purposeful way to travel and live abroad as it helps the person with a disability to experience the cultural aspects of another country through participating in the daily life of a community. It can also be combined with study, work, research and community service overseas.

NCDE has contacts with many disability organisations abroad. These may prove a good resource for finding accessible housing through their own disabled members. The accommodation may take the form of hosting or swapping homes with a person with a disability from another country.

MUISA also has an initiative called the Peer-to-Peer Network. This project gives individuals with disabilities who have participated in international programs the opportunity to share their experiences with others who are planning to participate.

The Institute on Independent Living

Peterséns Väg 2
127 41 Stockholm-Skärholmen Sweden
Tel: (8) 740 42 00   *Fax:* (8) 740 45 00
Email: ratzka@independentliving.org
http://www.independentliving.org/VacationHomeSwap.html

The purpose of The Institute on Independent Living is to promote the opportunities of persons with disabilities to gain more personal and political power, self-determination, full participation and equality through information, training materials, consultancy and technical assistance.

The Institute works in cooperation with other organisations which support these aims at the local, national and international level, including self-help groups in developing countries. It offers training materials, technical assistance and information on personal assistance, advocacy, access, legislation and peer support.

The Institute's web site has useful links to other disability resources.

Vacation Home Exchange is a service supported by the Institute and intended exclusively for persons with disabilities.

You may submit your listing on-line free of charge. Adverts should involve only apartments or homes which offer a certain degree of accessibility for persons with physical disabilities.

Like most of the fee-based exchange clubs, the service offers no guarantees. Vacation Home Exchange provides the contacts but does not assist in making any arrangements.

You may post a listing on their web site even if you don't have email facilities but, naturally, your quest for an exchange will be facilitated if you have an email address. Unfortunately, there are no facilities to allow you to edit your listing so you need to contact Adolf Ratzka at the address above to make the changes for you. This system seems to have led to some rather outdated listings remaining on the site.

You are requested to describe the accessibility features of your home in as much detail as possible. Listings without information on accessibility will not be included. In addition to the standard questions posed by exchange clubs, you will be asked the following:

- Are you or another member in your household physically disabled?

- Describe your home:

  General information

  Size in square feet or metres and number of rooms

- Describe things to do and how to get there from where you live

- Accessibility features of interest:

  In what way is your home or apartment accessible for disabled persons? (For example, state whether you yourself or another member of your household use a wheelchair and if so, which type.)

Describe wheelchair accessible transportation, if any, nearby or in the area.

Sample listings

Sydney, Australia

My 2-bedroom house is in the geographical centre of Sydney 40 min from coast close to shops trains and buses, suitable for 3–4 people near parks and golf course, very central close to Olympic site at Homebush. Hoping to swap for home close to St Petersburg, Russia, Finland for 6–8 weeks

Accessibility information:

I'm a quadriplegic so house is fully accessible shower, toilet, ramps, hoist, shower chair, kitchen, should also have a vehicle available. Some buses and trains accessible and taxis everywhere.

Utrecht, The Netherlands

We have a really nice 3-bedroomed semi suitable for 4–5 persons situated 5 miles from Utrecht in a green setting. Bikes, barbeque, computer, piano etc. Also two cats and two rabbits to be fed. Holland is great for accessibility if you have a car. Utrecht is delightful and there are some wonderful places to visit within easy driving distance of our home, with or without kids. Schiphol and Amsterdam are both 45 min drive. Zeist, our home town, is very attractive and has lots of shops, cinema, swimming pool, etc. We would like a coastal holiday in the UK for two or three weeks from 25 July. We are a family of 4; our daughters are 8 and 12 years old. My father, who is elderly, will be accompanying us. Our oldest daughter uses a manual wheelchair.

Accessibility information:

The ground floor and garden are accessible for wheelchair users. Our daughter uses a manual one. On the ground floor are a large bedroom and a bathroom with an adjustable sink, high toilet and shower. An adjustable bed is on order. We have no hoist. Upstairs is one bedroom with a double bed and one with two singles. We will be leaving our Citroen estate car at home but this is not adapted. Public transport is not friendly for wheelchair users in Holland, but nearly everything else is and people tend to be helpful and to speak English.

Youth Hospitality Exchange

An opportunity of a lifetime, Youth Hospitality Exchange provides young people with an affordable way to spend time in another country. The hospitality may be reciprocal or non-reciprocal. Whether yours is the host family or it is your youth enjoying the hospitality of another family, opportunities exist to help promote peace and understanding throughout the world by learning about other cultures.

Teenage brothers, Patrick and Ross, from Perth, Australia went to Dinan, Brittany on a two-week trip arranged through their school. The main objective of the homestay was to allow Australian students to attend a French school and experience family life in a French home.

The school has a long-standing arrangement with a local company who arranges homestays in Europe for students of private schools. They liaised with the Mayor of Dinan who sought expressions of interest from local people to act as host families.

The families were selected, in part, by their proximity to the participating French school. School teachers decided which students were suitable for the trip, a decision based primarily on behaviour at school rather than exam results. The school submitted a list of the participating students and the company matched them with an appropriate family.

The Australian school teachers, who were living with a friend close by, attended the school during the day. This allowed them to sort out any problems experienced by the boys. However, they didn't get involved in issues concerning the student/host family relationship.

The students were not given an opportunity to request a specific family. There were no provisions to deal with potential problems between students and their host families. This wasn't of concern because they were staying for such a short time. They were all very excited about living with a family they had never met before.

Responsibilities of host families

- provide board and lodging
- collect students from the railway station on arrival
- provide transportation to and from the school
- undertake some sight-seeing tours for students

Responsibilities of students

- must be currently studying French at school
- complete a medical questionnaire
- pay for airfares and associated costs for accompanying teachers
- display good manners and behaviour
- bring a gift for the family

The boys had this to say on their return: "*It was a wonderful experience. Staying in a youth hostel or hotel wouldn't have allowed us to really get to know French people. The experience allowed us to attend school where we made many new friends.*

The school held a welcome for us which made us feel very special. The French students were really interested to hear about life in Australia. Using French at school and at home gave us a great opportunity to improve our language skills. It was amazing how we adapted to speaking French, especially if the family didn't speak English.

It was interesting to meet up with your friends and hear about their host families. Because they were so different, we all had quite different experiences. We were able to observe the differences between our two school systems, the occupations and the food as well as see the beautiful countryside.

The only disadvantage of the program was that it was too short. We have made new friends and intend to keep in touch with them, perhaps not very regularly but at least we'll send them postcards and Christmas cards.

We would like to host a student from another culture, so that they could experience in Australia everything we experienced in France. Meeting people the same age is interesting and making new friends from the other side of the world is great fun. It would be good to return the favour and show foreign students what a great place Western Australia is."

THE BENEFITS

The benefits to the travelling youth include the chance to:

- gain firsthand experience of a different culture

- learn a foreign language

- make friends with people from all over the world

- gain an edge over other university or college applicants

As a host family, the benefits include:

- the pleasure and pride of being able to 'show off' your country

- opportunities for your children to meet and host a foreign guest

- opportunities to broaden your own horizons and enrich your life

- the enjoyment of having young people around for retired couples

- a chance to taste family life for childless couples
- an opportunity to 'bring the world to you' when you may be unable to travel yourself

LEARNING THE LANGUAGE

It is not necessary to be fluent in another language when you arrive. However, it will obviously make your transition easier and you will get more out of the exchange if you have done some preparation.

Once your destination is known, it would be a good idea to make some effort to learn the local language or to brush up on any existing skills.

Some host families enjoy the chance to practice their own foreign language skills but you should discourage your hosts from trying to communicate in English. You will learn more about a country and its culture if you understand the language. Through total immersion, you will gain more fluency. Avoid seeking out people who speak English. This may mean spending less time with any classmates or peers with whom you may be travelling.

HOW TO ARRANGE A YOUTH EXCHANGE

As with home exchange, there are various ways to go about arranging a youth exchange or homestay. You may have family, friends or other contacts living overseas with whom you can set up your own youth exchange plan. Alternatively, you can place your own advertisements in newspapers of the country of your child's choice.

Some high schools offer exchange programs. Expect to contribute towards the cost of the teachers' airfares and expenses as part of your own cost.

Many standard home exchange clubs claim to facilitate youth hospitality exchanges. However, you will more than likely find that the choice and selection available through these clubs is very limited. It may be worth noting your interest in a youth exchange agreement when listing your home with them if you are already considering a home exchange. If, however, your interest lies only with youth hospitality exchange, you may be better served by applying through a specialist organisation.

There are various organisations specialising in youth hospitality exchange. Some operate in a wide range of countries while others specialise in fostering relationships and promoting youth exchanges between just two countries. You will find some resources at the end of this chapter.

SELECTING A PROGRAM

There are various options available and your choices will be largely dependent on the length of time you wish to spend overseas and whether you intend to reciprocate the hospitality.

Some high schools facilitate homestays where no return hospitality is required. These are usually for short periods of between one and three weeks. Other organisations offer youth exchanges and homestays for one school term or one school year.

When selecting an organisation for a longer-term stay, make sure there is a system in place to deal with situations such as where you find yourself uncomfortable with your host family. If you select the Rotary Club, for example, you will be assigned a Rotary counsellor who is your friend and mentor. The counsellor will try to have you moved to a new family, and nobody's feelings will be hurt.

PREPARATION

Participants need to complete an application form well in advance of the intended departure date. Each organisation has its particular requirements and deadlines. Parents must also sign the application form.

Other items that may be required as part of your application include:

- passport size photos
- informal pictures of family, home and friends
- character references
- school reports
- a letter of introduction written in English
- medical examination records
- treatment permission forms
- registration fee (usually refundable if the applicant is not accepted)

RECEIVING CREDIT FOR SCHOOLING

Some schools will give credit or partial credit for studies undertaken abroad. In some cases, it may be necessary to make up missed courses when you return. Check with your local school officials for guidance.

HOSTING A YOUTH

Organisations look for families with a genuine interest in people of other countries, their language and customs, and a desire to promote understanding and friendship between people of different cultural backgrounds.

Your family needs to be flexible and have the capacity for welcoming a teenager into your home. The size, affluence and ages of the host family members are not important factors. Families with small children, childless couples, retirees or one-parent families can all successfully host exchange students.

Your guest will be included in all family activities as a functioning member of your family. They may be given certain responsibilities such as taking care of their room and sharing light duties with other members of the family which might include washing dishes, setting the table or preparing a meal. Your guest should not be expected to baby-sit on a steady basis or do heavy housework.

A separate bedroom is preferable but not essential provided there is sufficient room for storage of personal belongings with some privacy.

You need to provide an environment in which your guest can learn as much as possible about your country. You should be sensitive to your guest during the transition phase of settling in to the new surroundings.

Expect to have your home inspected for suitability by a representative of the organisation you select. Further visits may occur some time after your guest arrives.

FORMAL PROGRAM RESOURCES

The following are a few organisations to get you started.

Australian Lions

http://home.vicnet.net.au/~lionsyx/

All Lions Youth Exchange Programs depart in early December and return in late January. A range of destination countries is available.

Applicants must be between 16 and 22 years of age at the date of departure. They must undergo a medical examination, obtain a doctor's clearance and an indemnity form must be signed by a parent or guardian.

The Lions Program accepts applications from prospective host families to offer hospitality to visitors from many different countries. Both city and country hosts are sought to offer a balance of what Australia has to offer.

British German Connection

http://www.bgconnection.com

The aim of the British German Connection is to help young people in Germany and the UK to find out a little more about each other's country and about each other. They will put you in touch. Then the next step is up to you.

Their web site provides information about the politics, economics, environment, culture and society and many aspects of life in each country. It also has some useful links to other sites as well as details of opportunities available which allow youth to spend time in another country.

Rotary Youth Exchange

http://www.studentexchanges.org/

Children of Rotarians and non-Rotarians are eligible for Rotary Youth Exchanges. Opportunities are available in dozens of countries throughout the world. Some are very popular destinations, while others are relatively unfamiliar to students and parents. There may be a limited number of exchanges within each country, and some students may not be best suited for the countries they prefer. Preferences are accommodated if possible.

Age restrictions for long-term outbound students require that you be no older than 18 years, 6 months on departure. Some graduating seniors will still be eligible, but others will have passed the age limit. For those, the short-term summer exchange program may offer an alternative.

Rotary has recently introduced 'New Generations Exchanges' for college students. Typically, a team of five to 10 college students is led by a Rotarian to a foreign country for three to four weeks during the summer. A team from this destination country then sends a team to your community.

Rotary also has a program for college students called an 'Ambassadorial Scholarship'. If selected, Rotary sends you to study in a foreign country with all expenses paid including airfare, tuition, room and board.

Summer exchange

Participants spend three to four weeks during the summer exploring a different country with its unique culture and language. In return, they welcome their 'host brother or sister' into their home and country for three to four weeks during the summer. Participants make lifetime friends and have a lot of fun together exploring each other's country.

To participate you must:

• be 15 to 18 years old

• attend high school or be a graduating senior

• agree to host a foreign student in your home for three to four weeks

How much does it cost?

The Rotary Youth Exchange program is organized by caring volunteers to keep the cost affordable. Summer exchanges cost about US$250 plus airfares and spending money. Your fee includes accommodation with your host family, meals and health insurance.

Academic Year Exchanges

Rotary Exchange students reach into the hearts of other cultures to understand the differences which separate us as human beings.

Rotary Clubs in the USA and Canada sponsor high school students to study at a high school abroad and live with host families in a foreign country for an academic year. In return, a student from the destination country comes to an American or Canadian community for an academic year.

To participate you must:

• be 15 to 18.5 years old when school starts abroad

• attend high school

• have average or above average grades

How much does it cost?

The value of a Rotary Youth Exchange scholarship is estimated to be US$15,000, but due to the voluntary non-profit nature of Rotary, participants usually pay $1,500 plus airfares, passport, visa if required, and spending money. From a parent's perspective, it may be less expensive for your child to go abroad than to stay at home!

The host Rotary Club in the destination country provides meals and accommodation with one or more caring host families, free tuition, and a monthly allowance, which varies from $50 to $100 monthly, depending on the country.

Youth Exchange Service (YES)

http://www.yesint.com/
4575 MacArthur Court, Suite 830
Newport Beach, California 92660
Tel: (714) 955 0232 (800) 848 2121

Youth Exchange Service (YES) is a non-profit educational organization dedicated to world peace and understanding through intercultural exchange.

YES believes that, to live in peace, people of different countries must have an understanding of other cultures and ways of living. As a teenager, the best way to accomplish this is to become a part of an American family through the YES 'Students Abroad' program.

Youth Exchange Service offers two programs from which to choose, depending on the length of exchange required. The single term program runs from January to June and the year long program runs from August or September to June.

Both programs offer a rewarding experience with American family living and attendance at a nominated secondary school.

This experience is available throughout the United States, through the participating schools in each family location, for your education.

To participate you must:

- have a genuine interest in the proposed experience
- have a sense of responsibility
- display a level of maturity
- have the capacity to adjust to new situations
- be a good student and of excellent character
- be aged 15 to 18 years
- have a good knowledge of the English language
- pay for Administration Costs, Medical-Accidental Life Insurance and airfares
- submit a registration fee of US$500

The completed application papers should be submitted to one of the YES representatives in your country before 1 May for the year long program and 1 September for the one term program.

Resources

The following information is provided as a starting place from which you can make a comparison search for a company that best suits your needs.

The information was carefully confirmed to the best of the author's ability and deemed to be correct at the time of printing. However, it is not possible to verify certain of the services offered by the clubs until becoming a member. This includes whether the club supplies a newsletter or the extent to which custom matching services are provided.

In some cases, it could not be determined that the club's web site was secure for transmitting credit card details. The goodwill and integrity of the club owner have been relied upon to provide accurate information.

Inevitably things will change. Readers are encouraged to verify all the information provided before making any commitments. Many of the clubs advised that they have plans for significant upgrades such as language translation, inclusion of video clips and other useful features.

Phone numbers appear as dialed from within the country. If you wish to dial from outside that country, delete the 0 in the area code and prefix the number shown with the country code.

Key:

🔒	Secure payment	✉	Contact members before joining
🗎	Cheque option	🔍	Preview listings before joining
📖	Printed catalogue	💻	Electronic newsletter
👥	Custom matching		

AUSTRALIA

HomeExchange.Com   **Est: 1996**
www.HomeExchange-Australia.com
Contact: Chris Burgess **Email:** chris@HomeExchange-Australia.com
Suite 6, 25-27 Marine Parade   **Tel:** (03) 9537 1207
St. Kilda, Victoria 3182   **Fax:** (03) 9525 4795
Cost: US$30/12months, includes photo

See Head Office entry under USA for details

Homestay Worldwide   **Est: 1989**
www.homestay.com.au
Contact: Clotilda Smith   **Email:** info@homestay.com.au
P.O. Box 137, Caringbah   **Tel:** (02) 9544 0126
New South Wales 1495   **Fax:** (02) 9544 0511
Cost: cost & payment terms unclear

Specialise in homestay, farmstay & B&B accommodation for visiting students & holiday makers

---

Housesitworld   **Est: 1999**
www.housesitworld.com
Contact: Danny Raynel   **Email:** info@housesitworld.com
P.O. Box 1212 Gympie   **Tel:** (07) 5447 9290
Queensland 4570   **Fax:** (07) 5447 9290
Cost: house-sitters pay US$30 up to 12months; home-owners advertise free

Fee covers listings for as many areas as required with free amendments; online language translator

---

Intervac

www.intervac.com

Contact: Verena Olesch   **Email:** verena@theideasroom.com

76 Hayberry Street, Crows Nest   **Tel:** (02) 8904 1016

Sydney, New South Wales 2065   **Fax:** (02) 8904 1016

Cost: AU$160/12months for one directory/on-line listing; AU$25 for photo

Web site translated into French

Latitudes Home Exchange (Head Office)   Est: 1993

www.home-swap.com

Contact: Carol Henderson   **Email:** info@home-swap.com

P.O. Box 478, Mt. Lawley   **Tel:** (08) 9328 7408

Western Australia 6050   **Fax:** (08) 9328 7629

Cost: on-line service US$50/12months (comes with a guarantee); custom matching US$50 to register & US$250 matching fee

Business was firmly established before going on-line; pioneered the custom matching service; website translated into French, Italian, German & Spanish, network of multi-lingual staff around the globe; highly personalised service

---

Latitudes Home Exchange   Est: 1993

www.home-swap.com

Contact: Jenny Wood   **Email:** jenny@home-swap.com

P.O. Box 562, Caloundra   **Tel:** (07) 5491 2076

Queensland 4551   **Fax:** (07) 5491 2076

Cost: see above

See Head Office entry above for company details

Latitudes Home Exchange

Est: 1993

www.home-swap.com

Contact: Pat Cutts

Email: pat@home-swap.com

49 Timber Ridge Road, Yetholme

Tel: (02) 6337 5197

New South Wales 2795

Fax: (02) 6337 5197

Cost: see above

See Head Office entry above for company details

Maxlink's Australian Home Swap

www.maxlink.com.au/homeswap

Contact: not provided

Email: homeswap@maxlink.com.au

4/11 Kenworth Place, Brendale

Tel: (07) 3889 6800

Queensland 4500

Cost: AU$52; extra AU$25 for photo; updating your listing costs AU$20

The House Exchange Company

Est: 1999

www.house-exchange.modus.com.au

Contact: Jonathan Cavanagh

Email: HouseEx@modus.com.au

P.O. Box 1093, West Leederville

Tel: (08) 9388 9390

Western Australia 6007

Fax: (08) 9219 5103

Cost: AU$25/12months, includes photo - home exchange; AU$80/ 12months - commercial rentals; AU$27 - house-sitters

Home exchange, house-sitting services, commercial property rentals. Mission is to make exchanges easier for everyone

Travel Choice
www.ans.com.au/~sydney/pages/home.htm
Contact: not provided   **Email:** sydney@ans.com.au
Street address not provided
Sydney, New South Wales   **Fax:** (02) 9774 4185
Cost: AU$30

CANADA

Another-Home.com   **Est: 1998**
www.Another-Home.com
Contact: Serge Dugas   **Email:** info@Another-Home.com
CP 303, Succursale Ahuntsic, Montréal   **Tel:** (514) 331 0552
Québec H3L 3N8
Cost: US$35/12months, includes up to 4 photos

Free translation service English to French; specialise mostly in home
exchanges for France; offer a complete personalised service in English
or French with questions answered the same day received

Christian Home Xchange.com
www.christianhomexchange.com
Contact: not provided   **Email:** info@ChristianHomeXchange.com
P.O. Box 5775, Victoria
British Columbia V8R 6S8
Cost: US$30/12months

Club l'Antre-Amis   Est: 1995
www.antre-amis.com
Contact: Denise and Gérard Lemay   **Email:** info@antre-amis.com
53, rue D'Auteuil App. 6, Québec   **Tel:** (418) 694 1113
Québec G1R 4C2
Cost: free listings for non-Canadians seeking exchanges to Canada;
CA$50 (US$32) for Canadians; CA$80 (US$51) to list a rental property

Home exchanges & holiday home rentals in major European cities e.g.
Paris, London & Florence & in popular destinations such as Provence,
Tuscany & Andalousia. Web site & listings translated into English &
French

Global Home Exchanges   Est: 2000
www.4homex.com
Contact: Dennis & Joanna Chobater   **Email:** admin@4homex.com
6140 Kirsten Drive, Nanaimo   **Tel:** (250) 756 6177
British Columbia V9V 1J7
Cost: US$3/1month; US$12/6months; US$19/12months (money back
guarantees for longer listings)

Price includes unlimited number of photos; flexibility regarding listing
period; you make a bid for custom exchanges

Latitudes Home Exchange   Est: 1993
www.home-swap.com
Contact: Caroline Northfield   **Email:** caroline@home-swap.com
P.O. Box 206, Port Dover   **Tel:** (941) 761 1709
Ontario N0A 1N0   **Fax:** (941) 761 1709
Cost: on-line service US$50/12months (comes with a guarantee);
custom matching US$50 to register & US$250 matching fee

See Head Office entry under Australia for company details

Seniors Home Exchange   **Est: 1997**
www.seniorshomeexchange.com
Contact: not provided   **Email:** Admin@seniorshomeexchange.com
2107 Danforth Avenue, Suite 133
Toronto, Ontario M4C 1K1
Cost: US$50/36months, photo included

Exclusively for the over 50 age group

Swap Away   **Est: 2000**
www.swap-away.com
Contact: Jennifer Fletcher   **Email:** swapaway@homestead.com
P.O. Box 1623, Station B, Hull   **Tel:** (819) 777 9893
Québec J8X 3Y5   **Fax:** (819) 777 6220
Cost: US$37/12months, includes photo; renewals US$30; extra photo
US$3.50

Exclusively for non-simultaneous exchanges; people who own second
homes or apartments book time in each other's places. Translation
service French to English & English to French costs 20 cents per word

---

DENMARK

Apollo Home Exchange   **Est: 1974**
www.sima.dk/haneys
Contact: Erik Haney   **Email:** haney@nethotel.dk
Tulipanlunden 2, Eskebjerg   **Tel:** 5929 1630
DK 4593   **Fax:** 5929 1630
Cost: US$83 when exchange is confirmed

Custom matching service exclusively

ENGLAND

Holi-Swaps.Com   **Est: 1997**
www.holi-swaps.com
Contact: Maurice S. Clarke   **Email:** maurice@holi-swaps.com
Stanley House, 22 Paradise Street   **Tel:** (01788) 330054
Rugby, Warwickshire CV21 3SZ   **Fax:** (01788) 330056
Cost: £25 (US$35), includes photo

Two electronic newsletters: Trading Places – monthly for members; Fast
Trade - contains swap offers; branch in USA; free listing translations
into French, Italian, German, Spanish & Portuguese

HolSwap   **Est: 1999**
www.holswap.com
Contact: not provided   **Email:** admin@holswap.com
250 Portland Road, Hove   **Tel:** (01273) 324276
East Sussex   **Fax:** (01273) 324711
Cost: 3months free then £15 (US$25), includes 4 photos

Members may offer their property for rental as well as exchange.
Introduction of video clips of members' homes planned. Members can
opt to be contacted by non-members

HomeLink International   **Est: 1953**
www.homelink-international.co.uk
Contact: Heather Anderson   **Email:** exchange@homelink.org.uk
Linfield House, Gorse Hill Road   **Tel:** (01344) 842642
Virginia Water, Surrey GU25 4AS
Cost: £95

Find your local contact from this web site

Internet Home eXchange Club   **Est: 2000**
www.ihxc.com
Contact: Gavin Bellamy   **Email:** membership@ihxc.com
76 Bridge Farm Road, Uckfield
East Sussex
Cost: US$28 lifetime membership (will be annual following promotional period), includes photo

The organisation is run by teachers & although not exclusive to them, a large number of the members are educators

---

Latitudes Home Exchange   **Est: 1993**
www.home-swap.com
Contact: Tim Secrett   **Email:** tim@home-swap.com
16 Rowe Avenue, Peacehaven   **Tel:** (01273) 581793
East Sussex BN10 7PF   **Fax:** (01273) 581793
Cost: on-line service US$50/12months (comes with a guarantee); custom matching US$50 to register & US$250 matching fee

See Head Office entry under Australia for company details

Réseau international d'échange de foyer   **Est: 1996**
www.exchange-of-homes.com
Contact: Mark Siegrist   **Email:** mail@exchange-of-homes.com
7A The Green, Sutton Courtenay   **Tel:** (01235) 847094 (UK)
Oxon OX14 4AE   **Fax:** (815) 5506605 (USA)
Cost: US$39/12months, includes photo; translation service US$20 (your listing appears twice)

Home exchange, vacation rental, low-priced B&Bs & G"tes. Members can opt to allow non-members to contact them; correspondence available in 3 languages; web site translated into English, French, German, Spanish; free message board & electronic newsletter

Swap and Go   **Est: 2000**
www.swap-and-go.co.uk
Contact: Chris Leeves   **Email:** support@swap-and-go.co.uk
34 Sandford Road, Aldershot   **Tel:** (01252) 319318
Hampshire GU11 3AE   **Fax:** (01252) 319317
Cost: US$45/12months, includes photo

Relatively new service with plans for overseas expansion, newsletter & translation services

---

The Swop It Holiday Club   **Est: 1996**
www.swopit-hols.co.uk
Contact: Roger Keepax   **Email:** roger@swopit.demon.co.uk
P.O. Box 6097, Basingstoke   **Tel:** (01256) 841097
Hampshire RG22 4FQ   **Fax:** (01256) 841097
Cost: US$40 annual joining fee plus US$40 per holiday week taken

Includes yacht, motorhome and caravan exchange; plans to introduce a letting agency

---

Worldwide Home Exchange Club
www.wwhec.com
Contact: not provided   **Email:** david.gurdon@btinternet.com
18-20 London Road   **Tel:** (01892) 619300
Royal Tunbridge Wells, Kent TN1 1DA   **Fax:** (01892) 619311
Cost: £40/12months, one directory January plus supplement April, extra £10 photo

Directory service only, no on-line listings

FRANCE

Domus2Domus   **Est: 1999**
www.domus2domus.com
Contact: Frank Quinty   **Email:** contact@domus2domus.com
                                                          Tel: (0)6 81 26 78 38
Cost: free; plans to introduce a fee of US$42

Web site & listings translated into French & English. Monthly e-newsletter. Automatic email notification to matching parties. Members can create a web page with text & photos of their home to promote their offer

---

Echange vacances LGC92   **Est: 2001**
www.blue-home.com
Contact: not provided   **Email:** postmaster@blue-home.com
Echanges Vacances LGC92, 71 rue Médéric
F-92250 La Garenne-Colombes   **Fax:** (0)1 42 42 79 54
Cost: free; includes photo & up to 8 links

Web site & listings translated into French & English; plans for Spanish & German. Home & hospitality exchange, house-sitting, B&B, holiday home rentals

---

Echanges Bovilé
www.bovile.com
Contact: Jo'lle & Michel Boyer   **Email:** bovile@aol.com
321, avenue Sadi Carnot   **Tel:** (0)4 90 30 15 15
84500 Bollene
Cost: €68 one-time joining fee; €168 once the exchange offer is accepted. Joining fee refunded if no success

Custom matching service exclusively, plans to post all listings on web site in French & English

---

Echanges Homevasion   **Est: 2000**
www.homevasion.com
Contact: Christine Lenormand   **Email:** info@homevasion.com
Le Bas de Parfouru 14310   **Tel:** (0)2 31 77 79 05
Parfouru sur Odon   **Fax:** (0)2 96 89 14 87
Cost: €59 to join; €38-114 per custom exchange

Custom matching service exclusively offering high calibre homes
ranging from apartments in Paris to character homes in the pleasant
countryside. Web site & listings translated into French & English

---

WorldXchange
www.worldxchange.net
Contact: not provided   **Email:** joey@worldnet.fr
Cost: free; US$10-100 donation requested if you find the site or service
useful

GERMANY

Latitudes Home Exchange   **Est: 1993**
www.home-swap.com
Contact: Sabine Jacobs   **Email:** sabine@home-swap.com
Mengelestr. 8 89335   **Tel:** (0173) 9621535
Ichenhausen   **Fax:** (08221) 71628
Cost: on-line service US$50/12months (comes with a guarantee);
custom matching US$50 to register & US$250 matching fee

See Head Office entry under Australia for company details

ITALY

Family Links   Est: 1993

www.familylinks.it

Contact: Elisabetta Carlucci & Paola Corrado

Email: info@familylinks.it   **Tel:** (06) 85354524

                                                  Fax: (06) 85354524

Cost: US$50 annual fee; US$100 matching fee

Custom matching service exclusively. Offer home exchange, youth cultural exchanges & au pair placements. Web site translated into English & Italian; free translation English to Italian

---

Latitudes Home Exchange   Est: 1993

www.home-swap.com

Contact: Cristina Pagetti   **Email:** cristina@home-swap.com

Frazione Vairano 4 27018   **Tel:** (0382) 619025

Vidigulfo (PV)   **Fax:** (0382) 619891

Cost: on-line service US$50/12months (comes with a guarantee); custom matching US$50 to register & US$250 matching fee

🔒   🔍

See Head Office entry under Australia for company details

NETHERLANDS

Privak   Est: 1995

www.privak.nl

Contact: Marjan Bosman   **Email:** info@privak.nl

Molenstraat 5 NL – 5366   **Tel:** (0)412 462747

BT Megen   **Fax:** (0)412 462747

Cost: €27,5 one-time joining fee; €98 matching fee

Custom matching service exclusively. Owner offers B&B & arranges exchanges for disabled people in adapted Dutch homes. Information can be requested in Dutch, English, French & German

Stay4Free   Est: 1998
www.stay4free.com
Contact: not provided   Email: info@stay4free.com
Cost: free

Not primarily a home swapping club, but you can find a variety of ways to stay somewhere else for free. Web site translated into English & Dutch

---

NEW ZEALAND

Intervac   Est: 1950
www.intervac.com
Contact: Ketty Philips   Email: kettydavid@paradise.net.nz
54 McKinley Crescent   Tel: (04) 934 4258
Wellington 6002   Fax: (04) 934 4259
Cost: NZ$140 (US$55)/6months on-line access, includes photo; NZ$170 (US$67)/6months on-line access plus one printed directory; NZ$40 for subsequent editions; NZ$180 list a rental property

Web site translated into French

Kiwi Stays
www.kiwistays.com
Contact: Nicole Bishop & Associates   Email: info@kiwistays.com
Suite 5N, 220 Waiwhetu Road   Tel: (04) 570 0226
Lower Hutt   Fax: (04) 570 0322
Cost: NZ$129 (US$65)/12months; includes photo

Specialise in homely accommodation in New Zealand with a distinctively 'Kiwi' character; visitors to New Zealand can get a real taste of how Kiwis live

Latitudes Home Exchange   Est: 1993
www.home-swap.com
Contact: Joe Beattie   **Email:** joe@home-swap.com
2 Jane Gifford Place, Bucklands Beach   **Tel:** (09) 534 2408
Auckland 1704   **Fax:** (09) 534 2498
Cost: on-line service US$50/12months (comes with a guarantee); custom matching US$50 to register & US$250 matching fee

See Head Office entry under Australia for company details

NORWAY

European Holiday Home Exchange Club
www.prodat.no/ehhec
Contact: Ragnar Skarstein   **Email:** ehhec@online.no
Postbox 585 N-6801 Førde   **Tel:** 57 82 34 18
                                           Fax: 57 82 31 58
Cost: NOK 440 incl. VAT (US$48)

Web site translated into Norwegian, French, German & English

SCOTLAND

Home Exchange (Scotland)   **Est: 1990**
Contact: Allan & Anne Thomson   **Email:** hescotland@onetel.net.uk
'Rosebank', Carberry Road   **Tel:** (01333) 427950
Leven, Fyfe KY8 4JQ   **Fax:** (01333) 427950
Cost: £40 (US$70) annual registration fee; £80 (US$140) for introduction

Custom matching service exclusively, no on-line services. Provide a personalised matching, introduction & advisory service to exchange visitors to Scotland; all Scottish members are known personally to the owners & their properties visited; overseas members must supply references

Home Exchange Network
Est: 1999

www.oas.co.uk/homexchange

Contact: David R. Sakol

70 Broomfield Avenue, Newton Mearns

Glasgow G77 5JP

Email: exchange@oas.co.uk

Tel: (0141) 5718068

Fax: (0141) 5718069

Cost: £19.95 for 1st year, then optional Life Membership for another £19.95. Or Life Membership immediately for £29.95 (US$29-45)

Plans underway for new user input system allowing members to input & amend their own listing

---

SWEDEN

Intervac
Est: 1950

www.intervac.org

Contact: Karl & Ann-Christine Gemfeldt

Storskiftesvägen 32 SE 291 73

Önnestad

Email: info@intervac.se

Tel: (0)44 702 70

Fax: (0)44 768 30

Cost: US$111 for one directory/on-line listing with photo; US$50 on-line listing only

Web site translated into French; find your local contact from this web site

SWITZERLAND

Fair Tours   **Est: 1993**

www.fairtours.ch

Contact: Thomas Schwager   **Email:** fairtours@gn.apc.org

Postfach 615 CH-9001

St. Gallen

Cost: joining fee SFr.50 (US$40) carried over if no exchange found, introduction fee SFr.250 (US$180); reduced fee for overseas members seeking exchanges in Switzerland (US$130)

Custom matching service exclusively; many members become personal friends of the owners; members outside Switzerland are offered a free translation service & advice on public transport travel. You may make contact with proposed partners before submitting introduction fee

USA

Apartment Swap.com   **Est: 1998**

www.ApartmentSwap.com

Contact: Greg Bartalos   **Email:** swapmaster@apartmentswap.com

134 W. 58th Street # 807   **Tel:** (212) 757 4418

New York, New York 10019

Cost: US$4.95 voluntary donation via Pay Pal

Newsletter has subscribers from over 22 countries

Digsville   **Est: 2000**
www.digsville.com
Contact: Helen Bergstein   **Email:** helen@digsville.com
P.O. Box 106, Hoboken   **Tel:** (201) 795 5002
New Jersey 07030   **Fax:** (201) 792 5031
                                                   Toll-free: (800) 974 6860
Cost: 30-day free trial, then US$4.95/1month; US$29.95/12months; US$49.95/24months, includes up to 6 photos

Communication tools include Personalized Message Centre for retrieving, reviewing & saving contacts; Chat/lively Message Boards, U-Rate (unique rating system), stories from members (newsstand)

---

exchange places.com
www.exchangeplaces.com
Contact: not provided   **Email:** admin@exchangeplaces.com
1029 K Street, Suite 36   **Tel:** (877) 597 5223
Sacramento, California 95814
Cost: US$65/12months

Global Home Stays   **Est: 2001**
www.globalhomestays.com
Contact: Rebecca Benenson   **Email:** info@globalhomestays.com
3293 Jog Park Drive, West Palm Beach   **Tel:** (310) 995 0000
Florida 33467   **Fax:** (561) 433 1057
Cost: free - there are plans to introduce a fee of US$25/12months, includes photo

A meeting ground for travellers to find international friends with common interests for home swapping, homestays & travel companions. Assistance finding competitive airfares. Web site translated into French, German, Italian, Portuguese & Spanish

Home Exchange International
www.heig.com
Contact: not provided   **Email:** admin@heig.com
P.O. Box 1084, Canton
Connecticut 06019
Cost: free, but request that you become a subscribed member at US$35/ 12months should you engage in one or more exchange. Payment terms unclear

---

Home Free
www.homefree.com
Contact: not provided   **Email:** seattlek@uswest.net
Box 20566, Seattle   **Tel:** (206) 323 6169
Washington 98102-0301   **Fax:** (206) 323 6169
Cost: free for limited time, then US$45-95/12months

Find a travel companion

HomeExchange.Com (Head Office)   **Est: 1996**
www.HomeExchange.com
Contact: Roy Prince   **Email:** admin@HomeExchange.com
P.O. Box 30085, Santa Barbara   **Tel:** (805) 898 9660
California 93130   **Fax:** (805) 898 9199
Toll-free: (866) 898 9660
Cost: US$30/12months, includes photo

Web site translated into German, Italian, French, Spanish, Dutch & Danish. Listings available in over 60 countries. Associates in Italy & Australia. Electronic newsletter & web-based translation service planned

---

Hospitality Exchange   **Est: 1988**
www.goldray.com/hospitality
Contact: Wayne & Kathie Phillips **Email:** hospitalityex@hotmail.com
P.O. Box 561, Lewistown   **Tel:** (406) 538 8770
Montana 59457
Cost: US$20/12months;US$35/24months includes 2 directories (March & August/Sept) with your listing in one

A traveller's directory of friendly, travel-loving people who offer each other hospitality in their homes

---

International Home Exchange Network   **Est: 1995**
www.ihen.com
Contact: Linda Allen   **Email:** linda@ihen.com
P. O. Box 915253, Longwood   **Tel:** (407) 862 7211
Florida 32791   **Fax:** (407) 869 7992
Cost: US$29.95/12months, includes two photos

Can be invoiced for membership fee

Jewish Travel Network
www.jewish-travel-net.com
Contact: not provided   **Email:** info@jewishtravelnetwork.com
P.O. Box 283, San Carlos   **Tel:** (650) 368 0880
California 94070   **Fax:** (650) 599 9066
Cost: US$25, money back guarantee

Home exchange, homestay & hospitality listings, web site offers a meeting place for Jewish travellers

Latitudes Home Exchange   **Est: 1993**

www.home-swap.com

Contact: Michael Northfield   **Email:** michael@home-swap.com

P.O. Box 622, Cortez   **Tel:** (941) 761 1709

Florida 34215   **Fax:** (941) 761 1709

Cost: on-line service US$50/12months (comes with a guarantee); custom matching US$50 to register & US$250 matching fee

See Head Office entry under Australia for company details

SunSwap.com

www.sunswap.com

Contact: not provided   **Email:** info@sunswap.com

P.O. Box 159, Lyme

New Hampshire 03768

Cost: US$39.95/12months, includes photo

The VacationExchange Network   **Est: 1996**

www.thevacationexchange.com

Contact: Bernard Bloomfield

Email: sales@thevacationexchange.com

11 Parrott Drive, Parsippany   **Tel:** (973) 386 9208

New Jersey   **Fax:** (973) 428 3925

                                Toll-free: 1-800-CONDO-44

Cost: US$10 annually/US$75 when exchange is secured, includes photo, each additional photo US$5

Specialise in vacation properties at some of the best resort areas. All properties are vacation homes so exchanges need not be synchronised

Trading Homes   Est: 1991
www.trading-homes.com
Contact: Ed Kushins   **Email:** info@trading-homes.com
P.O. Box 787, Hermosa Beach   **Tel:** (310) 798 3864
California 90254   **Fax:** (310) 798 3865
                                     Toll-free: 1-800-877-TRADE
Cost: US$65/12months on-line membership only or US$95 includes 3
directories; unlimited on-line photos, text & links included

Web site translated into French & Italian. Message board allows
questions & comments for other exchangers. Weather & tourism links
on each listing; 'save' interesting listings on 'my trading home' page &
'notify me' feature when suitable listings are added. Plans for a chat
room & email newsletters

Vacation Point Exchange   Est: 2001
www.vacationpointexchange.com
Contact: Mary Puskar   **Email:** info@vacationpointexchange.com
P.O. Box 591049, Houston   **Tel:** (281) 218 9455
Texas 77259   **Fax:** (425) 940 1489
Cost: Pay a per night fee from US$25-65 determined by the rental value
of the property

A network of second home, B&B & Inn owners. Members trade time in
their property for points for use at another member's vacation property

WALES

HouseSwaps.com
www.houseswaps.com
Contact: not provided   **Email:** info@houseswaps.com
Cost: £21 (US$30)

Holiday exchanges using your home, boat, caravan, motor home or trade your timeshare weeks

Glossary

.jpeg the extension used for graphics files in the JPEG format

browser a program that lets you read HTML documents and navigate around the Web

CD Compact Disc, a small, portable, round medium for electronically recording, storing and playing back audio, video, text and other information in digital form

CD ROM Compact Disc, read-only-memory, an adaptation of the CD designed to store computer data in the form of text, graphics and hi-fi stereo sound

consecutive exchange series put into position two or more separate home exchange arrangements in successive order

custom matching tailor-made home exchange arrangements facilitated by a home exchange club

directory service cataloguing of member listings by a home exchange club for distribution to its members by printed or electronic means

domestic exchange a home exchange within your own country

eco-tourism a form of tourism in which tourists are ecologically and culturally sensitive to minimising their impact, where learning is a key element and which is of benefit to local communities

email electronic mail, a system that allows messages to be sent and received via a computer

frequent flyer program program offered by airlines whereby customers are rewarded for their loyalty which can take the form of complimentary flights, flight upgrades, car rentals, hotel accommodation or passes to related tourist attractions

FTP File Transfer Protocol, a protocol defining how files are transferred from one computer to another; also a program used to move files

home exchange the reciprocal exchange of the use of homes by two parties for a temporary period

home exchange club an organisation which facilitates home swapping

home swap club see home exchange club

home swapping the reciprocal exchange of the use of homes by two parties for a temporary period

homestay a variation on hospitality exchange, usually a non-reciprocal arrangement whereby board and lodging is provided with an established host. Not free but the costs are generally cheaper than traditional forms of accommodation

hospitality exchange participants offer hospitality at their home in return for reciprocal hospitality at a later date

host agent the agent or branch office of a home exchange club which has enlisted a specific property for exchange

house-sitter wanted free lodging offered in return for services to carry out basic home and garden maintenance and pet care

house-sitting offered participants offer their services to stay in a home, carry out basic home and garden maintenance and may include pet care in return for free lodging

HTML Hypertext Markup Language, a coding language used to create Web documents

hyperlink a connection between two Web documents, usually a text or picture that can be clicked on to instruct a browser to display another Web document

Internet a worldwide network of computer networks that evolved from the Advanced Research Projects Agency of the US Department of Defence

internet computer networks connected to one another (of which The Internet is an example)

interstate exchange a home exchange between people living in a different state, province or county within the same country

intrastate break a home exchange, usually of short duration such as a long weekend or during a national holiday, between people living in the same state, province or county

ISP Internet Service Provider, a company that provides a connection to the Internet

keywords characteristic words or phrases used to conduct a search and used by search engines to find and categorise a Web page

link see hyperlink

listing a property registered for a home exchange

navigate to move around the Web using a browser

non-reciprocal exchange accommodation hospitality which is either not repaid or is countered by hospitality from a third party

scanner a device that attaches to a computer and captures images such as house photographs for computer editing and display. Usually comes with software that allows resizing and modification of a captured image

search engine a program that creates a huge index using various criteria for determining the most important sites from pages that have been read; a program that receives your search request, compares it to the entries in the index and returns results to you

Secure Socket Layer transactions (SSL) encryption technology that ensures your information, including credit card details, is protected during transmission

snail mail slang term for the regular postal service with the implication that it is much slower than email

SSL see Secure Socket Layer transactions

transaction combination the use of a home or hospitality exchange as only one component of the total accommodation means

unsynchronised exchange a home exchange between two parties travelling on different time schedules

URL Uniform Resource Locator, a Web address

web page see web site

web site a collection of Web documents about a particular subject

World Wide Web a hypertext system that allows users to travel through linked documents following any chosen route

www see World Wide Web

youth hospitality exchange a teenager stays with a host family overseas in return for reciprocal hospitality for the teenager of that family

Index

A

additional guests, 111, 118
advertising, 61
agreement, 32, 78, 106, 108, 110, 122, 124, 126, 166, 170. *See* contract
appliances, 86, 99, 100, 119, 129, 153, 154
authentic local culture, 7, 20

B

benefits, 5, 6, 16, 19, 23, 24, 27, 45, 182

C

car exchange, 119, 120, 121, 127. *See* swapping cars
children, 9, 12, 18, 23, 24, 75, 76, 79, 85, 97, 100, 118, 127, 130, 131, 132, 164, 166, 172, 182, 186
communication tips, 105
contingency plans, 122, 123, 129
contract, 77. *See* agreement
custom matching, 32, 39, 64, 73, 74, 78, 79, 174, 215
Custom Matching Service Contract, 77

D

destinations, 10
disability, 175, 176, 177
disabled traveller, 13, 98
drawbacks, 28

E

eco-tourism, 16, 26, 215
email, 58, 59, 65, 66, 67, 68, 74, 81, 82, 100, 103, 104, 105, 215, 218
exchange guests, 6, 26, 30, 44, 86, 92, 103, 112, 114, 115, 118, 119, 121, 124, 130, 132, 153, 164, 165, 168, 169. *See* exchange partners
exchange partners, 5, 8, 10, 11, 19, 21, 25, 27, 29, 34, 35, 40, 41, 42, 78, 89, 90, 91, 92, 100, 101, 103, 104, 112, 113, 115, 117, 119, 120, 122, 123, 124, 126, 132, 152, 165, 167, 170. *See* exchange guests

F

fact file, 88, 160. *See* information file
Fact File for Exchange Guests, 155

G

gardening, 125, 128, 154
guidelines, 2, 66, 70, 78, 111

H

home exchange, 1, 2, 3, 9, 10, 17, 31, 36, 41, 45, 52, 54, 60, 62, 87, 90, 91, 109, 118, 127, 137, 152, 160, 184, 215, 216, 217, 218. *See* home swapping
Home Exchange Agreement form, 127
home exchange club, 2, 215. *See* home exchange clubs

home exchange clubs, 48, 50, 62, 80, 184. *See* home exchange club
home swapping, 4, 5, 8, 9, 12, 16, 27, 28, 35, 39, 58, 60, 62, 63, 66, 79, 83, 84, 86, 91, 216. *See* home exchange
homestay, 48, 176, 180, 184, 216
hospitality exchange, 13, 45, 47, 52, 184, 216, 218
host amenities, 16, 24
house-keeping, 28, 30, 160, 170
house-sitting, 50, 51, 216

I

information file, 152, 153. *See* fact file
insurance, 17, 18, 111, 118, 119, 120, 121, 122, 123, 129, 134, 189
internet listing, 64

K

keys, 29, 43, 114, 127, 149, 162, 167, 168

L

language, 31, 32, 48, 52, 80, 130, 167, 181, 182, 183, 186, 188, 191
letter of introduction, 57, 75, 88, 89, 90, 173, 185
linens and towels, 117, 128, 166

M

maintenance, 13, 111, 117, 121, 154

N

non-reciprocal, 45, 47, 180, 216

P

pet care, 16, 23, 124, 125, 129
photographs, 6, 9, 29, 57, 59, 62, 75, 217. *See* photos
photos, 59, 65, 88, 89, 105, 165, 185. *See* photographs
printed directory, 64, 69, 70, 71, 133
private listing, 73

R

rental, 18, 52, 103
repairs, 117, 121, 125, 128, 157, 167
retirees, 12, 55, 98, 186

S

Sample Instruction Sheet, 160
sample letters, 106
second home, 48, 49, 110, 123, 153, 168
swapping cars, 19. *See* car exchange

T

telephone bills, 50, 54, 114, 127

U

unlisted membership, 73
unsynchronised exchange, 123, 218
utility bills, 50, 116, 127, 135

W

World Wide Web, 64, 218

Y

youth hospitality, 180, 184, 218
youth hospitality exchange. *See* youth hospitality